◼ The Special Child

Books by Robin White

House of Many Rooms (1958)
Elephant Hill (1959)
Men and Angels (1961)
Foreign Soil (1962)
All in Favor Say No (1964)
His Own Kind (1967)
Be Not Afraid (1972)
The Special Child (1978)

▣ The Special Child

A Parents' Guide to Mental Disabilities

ROBIN WHITE

Little, Brown and Company   Boston   Toronto

COPYRIGHT © 1978 BY ROBIN WHITE

FIRST EDITION

T 8/78

LIBRARY OF CONGRESS CATALOGING IN PUBLICATION DATA

White, Robin, 1928-
   The special child.

   Bibliography: p.
   1.   Mentally handicapped children.   2.   Mentally
handicapped children—Care and treatment.   3.   Mentally
handicapped children—Family relationships.   I.   Title.
HV891.W48   362.7′8′3   78-5656
ISBN 0-316-93597-2

Designed by Susan Windheim

Published simultaneously in Canada
by Little, Brown & Company (Canada) Limited

PRINTED IN THE UNITED STATES OF AMERICA

For Checkers, my son,
who stood in a field unknown,
showing the way.

◉ Acknowledgments

For their helpful suggestions in the preparation of this book, I wish to express my deep appreciation to: Ellsworth T. Neumann, M.D., Vice-President, The Rockefeller Foundation; Richard Koch, M.D., Children's Hospital in Los Angeles; Gunnar Dybwad, Ph.D., Brandeis University; Frank Menolascino, M.D., President, National Association for Retarded Citizens; Raymond M. Peterson, M.D., Director, San Diego Regional Center; William T. Gray, former Director, North Coast Regional Center; Grady Fort, M.D., Chief, NCRC Medical Services; Judy Lechowick, NCRC Nutritionist; Llewellyn Howland III, Little, Brown and Company; and Marian B. White, my wife.

For their encouragement, my thanks to: Bernard Rimland, Ph.D., Director, Institute for Child Research in San Diego; Lendon H. Smith, M.D., Portland, Oregon; Laura W. Neville, M.D., New York Upstate Medical Center; Benjamin F. Feingold, M.D., Kaiser Medical Center in San Francisco; Hugh Brown, Ph.D., University of Miami; Morris A. Wessel, M.D., New Haven, Conn.; and Merrill S. Read, Ph.D., World Health Organization.

For informational assistance, I have been aided by: Epilepsy Foundation of America, National Association for Retarded Citizens, Developmental Disabilities Technical Assistance System, National Institute of Mental Health, *Modern Medicine* magazine, and William J. Green, Director, California Association for the Retarded.

And for their abundant care throughout, I am grateful to: James Oliver Brown, Mathilde K. Biesterfeld, Ruth and Emmons White, and my special partisans, Parker White and Shelley Kumar.

Note on Style

To facilitate the ease of reference preferred by many families, in-line sources have been noted where necessary and the publishers' information omitted for simplification, until listed under *Recommended Reading*.

Contents

The Myth of Normality   3
*The importance of how we perceive
each other*

Prevention   23
Avoiding developmental disabilities

Early Care   47
Basics of infant stimulation

Later Detection   69
What to look for and do

The Parents   90
Ways to lighten burdens

Brothers and Sisters   109
The other special children in need

Education   129
Reducing pressures for teacher and pupil

Adolescence   148
Improving psychosexual development

Therapy   161
*Enhancing independence for the
young adult*

CONTENTS

Nutrition and the Environment   183
    Reducing stress in the way we live
Society   197
    A program for eliminating fears
Agencies   208
Recommended Reading   211
Biographical Note   217

■ The Special Child

◙ The Myth of Normality

Where shall wisdom be found?
And where is the place of understanding?
—*Book of Job*

DURING THE PAST TEN YEARS, A WEALTH OF INFOR-mation has been amassed about the mystery of brain disabilities that occur in developing children. Although much of it seemed beyond reach of the untrained person, we are beginning to realize that there are many things families can do to help themselves, *after* medical care, by understanding what is involved.

As parents of a multiply handicapped son, my wife and I have learned a great deal over two decades, working with organizations and studying research available to us. This book is an attempt to convey what we know in a usable way for others expecting or caring for children, so that all may seize initiatives in trying to bring about the optimum evolution of humanity.

From personal experience, I can well appreciate the fact that one problem with information about brain impairment up to now relates to division of the subject according to symptom, which tends to isolate each condition by category. In turn, parents of an afflicted child often feel alone or in the dark. To cast some light on things, anywhere from three to ten percent of the population have some form of identified brain handicap.

Perhaps twice as many may also be affected, yet manage to go unnoticed.

Such a range in percentage reflects the way various facets of the mind are studied by different groups, who compile their own statistics. Simply totaling all these numbers does not give a reliable picture, as noted by the 1974 Research Task Force Report of the National Institute of Mental Health, which places the incidence of brain disorders at one in ten. After screening for overlap, *at least* three of every one hundred children have a diagnosed "developmental disability" — retardation, epilepsy, cerebral palsy or autism. But in its full sense, the term applies to many conditions that limit the brain during growth, from conception to maturity. So if all types are included, such as minimal brain dysfunction (MBD), the figure may rise to around ten percent, not counting the even higher numbers involved in later injury, as well as biochemical errors that can result in some prevalent forms of mental illness.

At best, reaching an exact measure is difficult. The National Association for Retarded Citizens reports that six million Americans, or three percent of the population, are retarded. The Epilepsy Foundation of America holds that two percent, or four million people in the United States, have some form of seizures. In its June 7, 1976, issue, the *Journal of the American Medical Association* quoted the incidence of MBD as three to ten percent, while other estimates run from five to twenty-eight percent of schoolchildren. The extent of reduced brain development because of poor nutrition is not known, though medical centers at the University of California and elsewhere indicate that several million are at risk. And some researchers suggest that total statistics may be very much higher than we presently realize, since lesser problems in the central nervous system often go unreported.

Whatever percentiles we agree to, it should in any event be clear that brain handicap has substantial implications. Yet despite the fact that almost half the hospital beds nationally are occupied by mental patients, we tend to regard brain malfunctions as relatively uncommon and hold to the myth of normality without first deciding what is meant by "normal" — how valuable or possible it is. Each of us is, after all, made different by even the ordinary things that happen in childhood.

The dictionary defines normal as "conforming to an established standard or common type" — whatever appears average for a given culture and period. Presumably, if one equals or exceeds minimum standards, that is normal; if for any reason one falls below, that is abnormal. To some, the mental capacity of athletic heroes interviewed on television might seem doubtful. To others, genius can look a bit different. And many of us are apt to decry as deficient the advocates of opposing views. But who is final judge? What characteristics are to be accepted or rejected?

The following traits describe three people:

Social	Unsocial	Oversocial
Attractive	Ugly	Hairy
Generous	Greedy	Spendthrift
Loving	Fearful	Delusional

5

Cooperative	Mean	Flamboyant
Talented	Crafty	Tricky
Neat	Sloppy	Fat

Which one would be welcome as a guest?

The left column belongs to a retarded boy who plays the banjo, the center column to Charles Dickens's Scrooge, the right column to our celebrated Santa Claus. All traits are interpretive, beauty determined by the beholder, and none is a fixed entity. Some people are more loving, or more fearful; pleasing qualities differ; every capacity changes. What is dominant one day may be recessive the next. So, on the basis of appearances, do we approve of each other on normal days and shoot it out on the abnormal — losing, not using, our heads?

Solving any problem begins by trying to understand it, and injury — or, as it is sometimes called, "insult" — to the brain is serious for a number of reasons, over and above the physical. First, it is a complex aberration that requires cooperative response by several professions. Second, there is often a compounding negative reaction to the symptoms. And third, the causes vary widely, as do the terms used to describe the results.

By way of comparison, when someone breaks a leg, the bone is set by the doctor, recovery is expected, the injured person sympathized with, and the injury called "a broken leg." But when something goes wrong in the brain, effective treatment involves doctor, psychologist, social worker, teacher and family; recovery projections cannot encourage premature optimism; the patient faces social difficulties and is called one or more things, depending upon who made the initial diagnosis. Despite evident differences, the person is then special-grouped as "exceptional." While this term may be a vast improvement over earlier ones, it tends to suggest that everyone else is average and to imply that the exceptional are somehow alike, when *no* two people are the same, and we *all* have special needs.

Schizophrenia, for instance, is said by some to have its basis in biochemical misfire, resulting in a thought-process disorder that is an organic brain malfunction. With waking perceptions and dream sleep modified, the individual experiences a separation between feelings and reality — as happens when we see a movie and are still gripped by emotions long after the show is over. Yet what may be a biochemical difficulty is generally ascribed to some omission by the mother. The victim is confined and sedated, which further alters dream sleep, and the symptoms are treated instead of the cause, even though psychiatrists, beginning with Freud, have had little success trying to talk it away.

At times, society seems to have invested the brain with an aura of superstition. Perhaps this is not surprising in view of history. The ancients believed that there was a relation between silver and the moon, that brain problems were caused by lunar influences, thus giving rise to the word "lunacy" and the use of silver in treatment (until the nineteenth century, silver nitrate was prescribed for epilepsy). Although Hippocrates correctly identified the origin of convulsive disorders, his observation was largely disregarded for two thousand years. Aristotle held that the brain was for cooling blood. Early literature, including the Bible, has many references to using divine exorcism on those with mental disabilities. Li T'ieh-Kuai, the Iron Crutch Immortal from the Chin Dynasty myths and legends, was believed capable of leaving his body at times — a visible sign of petit mal (one type of epilepsy in which a person has periodic lapses of consciousness). In primitive tribes, medicine men practiced magic to release the spirit thought to be possessing someone whose behavior was considered different or variable. Undoubtedly, many brain-handicapped people were looked upon as spellbound (the word "spell" remains extant today in describing certain mental manifestations). Numerous stories of the supernatural may have been inspired by the nighttime activities of afflicted persons confined during the day. And for a substantial period of modern history, the asylum was no fiction at all — perhaps one reason why Van Gogh lived alone, cared for by his brother, after syphilis began disordering his mind, as it did that of Randolph Churchill, father of Winston. When George Washington's stepdaughter, Martha Parke Custis, developed epilepsy at age twelve, doctors had her wear an iron ring supposedly endowed with curative occult powers. The invalidism of Ida Saxton McKinley, wife of the President, was simply kept from the public and explained as attacks of fainting. And Mark Twain ambitiously sought help in Europe for his daughter but was unable to remedy her convulsions, though in 1857 Sir Charles Locock had discovered the first known anticonvulsant: salts of bromide.

In more recent years, brains have been treated with

electricity and psychosurgery (destruction or direct stimulation of healthy tissue by any means to alter behavior). Frontal lobotomy did not fall into disuse until the 1950s. As late as 1960, the fact that someone had to see a psychiatrist was hushed up to avoid loss of job or social standing. Even today, we are apt to refer not to the brain but to the heart, gut and spleen as the centers of feeling, determination and mood, or to regard the attributes of "personality" and "spirit" as being unrelated to mind.

But the main roadblock to progress with developmental disabilities followed the widespread acceptance of Mendel's laws around the turn of the century. Using peas, an Austrian monk, Gregor Johann Mendel, was able to demonstrate the way dominant and recessive physical characteristics, such as size and shape, were inherited. When investigators applied these laws to people, they utilized mental institutions, thus in a sense "discovering" the asylums but, without scientific controls, drawing the conclusion to fit the premise: that all brain handicap was a sign of family taint whose elimination would enable mankind to breed perfection. This view led to widespread shame and concealment, effectively putting research into limbo for fifty years. By the 1920s, most states had passed laws mandating the sterilization of the afflicted and denying them rights guaranteed under the Constitution. In turn, legal segregation contributed to the rise of stereotypes and to rigidity in public attitudes concerning the developmentally disabled.

One problem with the genetic approach is that it tends

to treat life, like Latin, as a dead language: unchanging and therefore absolute. Fortunately, the only workable definition of life *is* change, evolution meaning genetic flexibility. As nutritionist Dr. Myron Winick of Columbia has observed, today we realize that "the number of cells present in any organ at maturity is only partially under genetic control." (*Malnutrition and Brain Development.*) But for some reason, those who believed that there were no diseases, only susceptible bodies — a statement not unlike claiming that there are no robbers, only susceptible houses — failed to observe that despite inhumane measures, the incidence of mental disorders remained unchanged. Similarly, genetic purification by the Nazis to achieve the master race took the premise to an extreme with the same result.

Apart from the limitation of institutional studies, which draw from marginal samplings in a restricted environment and cannot measure the impact of sensory deprivation, sexual segregation, poor nutrition and other matters pertinent to accurate case histories, investigators disregarded the influence of pellagra, caused by lack of niacin and resulting in mental changes, and the relation of epilepsy to cerebral birth lesions. Nor did they record the prevalence of hypoglycemia, a low level of glucose in the blood that leads to mental disturbances, or show any interest in the biochemistry of genetic damage. But above all, their assumptions did not take into account the fact that for the people involved, the problem is *here*, the problem is *now*, and help can only be prefaced by compassion.

By the 1960s, however, hope visibly emerged on a

broad front, after years of concerned effort, as parents and others began succeeding in their demand for legal, medical, educational and social reforms. Not long after enormous response to personalized articles in major national magazines, the Kennedys made public the retardation of their eldest daughter. It was revealed that one of the Dionne Quintuplets suffocated at night because of congenital epilepsy. And President Kennedy moved to enact change. The sequence is more complex than can be briefly summarized, and it would be impossible to identify the remarkable contributions of everyone involved, but archaic laws were weeded out, new laws were passed; research and service programs grew, backed by the 1970 Federal Developmental Disabilities Act, which pointed to de-institutionalization of brain handicap. This was followed by the 1973 Federal Rehabilitation Act, requiring that the most severely disabled be taken first to avoid the practice of "creaming," or serving only easy cases to make the data on progress and results look good. Two years later, the promising Health Services Act broadened the scope of care.

Slowly, benefits to mankind are being realized — perhaps too slowly for some parents, who still face difficulty obtaining coordinated assistance. A lot of outstanding people are working in all areas of this field — physicians, teachers, nutritionists, biochemists, family planners, counselors, psychologists. But they haven't yet fully gotten together — much as they may wish to — and funding remains piecemeal, with no requirement that resulting research information be integrated. Each family thus goes through the process of trying to find out what and where are the appropriate services. As Barry Kaufman records in *Son-Rise*, he and his wife, Suzi, searched tirelessly to help their autistic infant, Raun, and were refused by those who advocated early intervention but were reluctant to practice it until the boy was three or four.

On occasion, the search only consumes time and money to arrive at an incorrect diagnosis, as we have learned through our own experience and confidential contact with others. For example, consider the case of a young boy with cerebral palsy. Physically unable to get around, he was in trouble: both stamina and morale were low. So was his IQ score. At length, he was pronounced retarded and sent to a sheltered workshop, where the staff, beginning with the obvious, concentrated on improving his stamina through nutrition and exercise. Subsequent retesting then showed his IQ to be 130 and opened the way to new programs for him in order to make best use of his abilities. Within the year, he was attending school in the mornings, enjoying afternoon work and recreation to continue his physical progress. How exciting to ponder the possibilities of future contributions to society by this once "lost" human being!

In another instance, a brain-handicapped child was thought deaf until a curious social worker discovered that wax in her ears, accumulated over the years, had gone unnoticed. In yet another, the daughter of a prostitute had been neglected and underfed from birth, had developed a speech impediment, and was diagnosed as severely retarded. The local welfare agency then placed her in a group home associated with an activity center. At the center, she was helped to eat properly. Slowly, her speech began to clear up, revealing that she was not retarded, could handle complex tasks, learn to live independently.

Now, these children are *important*. Not only are they answers to an ancient riddle of the mind and our understanding of many complexities, from memory to learning and behavior, upon which rests the future of mankind, they are important because they *are*. Yet oversights about them can occur, especially in treatment of minority groups, where clues may be missed through lack of time, the pressures of an exhausting caseload or other problems, including communications. Children have been thought schizoid because of language conflicts arising from the mother's inability to speak English. In some situations, first-rate care has faltered owing to simple lack of information at the family level.

Despite such difficulties, the total picture is one that might best be characterized as "coming alive." What we see is a remarkable shift in outlook. Where once a sense of finality surrounded diagnosis of brain-handicapping conditions, we now find hopeful advances, championed by some of our most brilliant professionals, who are learning increased respect for the observations of parents and others, as well as encouraging cooperation among specialties to benefit the patient. Also, the vast evidence indicates that developmental disabilities are far from a fixed state. The IQ can be improved, epilepsy controlled, cerebral palsy helped in many cases, learning disabilities worked with, and the families involved substantially aided when comprehensive programs are available.

Of the many forms of developmental brain impairment, let me list some of the major ones that may or may not be associated:

Retardation — mild, moderate or severe difficulty in learning.

Epilepsy — more than sixteen types, ranging from convulsions to minor blackouts.

Cerebral palsy — reduced voluntary muscle control.

Autism — infantile withdrawal into self.

Learning disabilities

Aphasia — difficulty with language and comprehension.

Agraphia — impaired ability to write.

Alexia — reading confusion.

Hyperkinesia — physical overactivity with shortened attention span.

Chorea — involuntary movements, also known as St. Vitus's Dance.

Dystonia — muscular rigidity.

Spina bifida — open lesion at base of spine.

Cretinism — deformity due to absent or low thyroid.

Mongolism — congenital malformation due to chromosomal error.

While each of these terms has different implications, the purpose of citing them together is to underscore the need for a comprehensive approach to brain-handicapping conditions: we seem to have a multiplicity of words to describe *how* the mind is affected, to the point of sometimes losing sight of *what* is affected. However, those most commonly recognized and referred to as developmental disabilities continue to be retardation, epilepsy, cerebral palsy and autism, so a fuller understanding of each may prove useful.

The mentally retarded are people who have reduced ability to learn. Some manifest a sweet disposition that has led them to be called "nature's innocents." Others may have compounding emotional or physical problems, with attendant behavioral difficulties. It is widely accepted that around eighty percent of retardation is caused by socioenvironmental factors, such as chemical irregularities, poor maternal nutrition during pregnancy and lactation, malnutrition in infancy, viruses, head injury or poisons (such as lead). An estimated ninety percent of retardation is mild enough to permit the individuals to be educated, find work and live in the community. Those moderately retarded can be trained to care for themselves and perform tasks in a sheltered environment, while the severely retarded often have other handicaps that require more specialized assistance. But most are helped, like any of us, by a general improvement of the quality of life and opportunity, as the National Association for Retarded Citizens has been so exemplary in demonstrating.

Epilepsy, on the other hand, is an electrical misfiring of brain cells that usually does not affect intelligence and is characterized by episodes ranging from grand mal convulsions to petit mal loss of consciousness. The causes also vary: brain injury, biochemical imbalances, nutritional deficits, high fevers, infections of the central nervous system, brain tumors and some poisons. The U.S. Department of Health, Education, and Welfare estimates that fifty percent of those with epilepsy achieve complete control with anticonvulsant medication, while thirty percent experience partial control, which suggests that we need research to find new ways of helping redress the balance. Public attitude, for centuries based on myth, is slowly becoming more realistic, thanks to efforts by the Epilepsy Foundation of America and others. But many patients still face personal, social and economic uncertainties; effective assistance still involves integrated counseling in these areas, as well as balanced medication.

Cerebral palsy refers to brain dysfunctions that impair muscular and sensory abilities. The three main types are spastic, athetoid and ataxic. The spastic type is characterized by stiffness, the athetoid by uncontrolled movements, and the ataxic by reduced sense of balance. A major cause of palsy can be anoxia, or too little oxygen reaching the fetal brain. Other possible causes include poor maternal health and nutrition during pregnancy, injury to or infection of the central nervous system, and blood-type incompatibility between parents. While cerebral palsy is not necessarily associated with mental retardation, with some cases being almost unnoticeably slight, the person may have one or more other handicaps, such as epilepsy, sight and hearing problems, emotional difficulties. Many can be greatly helped by early diagnosis, treatment and stimulation to develop their physical and mental potentials. As a measure of progress being made, and the continuing efforts of United Cerebral Palsy, people with this affliction were once considered hopeless but today hold jobs in a wide variety of occupations.

For autism, which can occur in any social class and is generally defined as infantile withdrawal into self, there is no identified cause or agreed-upon mode of treatment. However, in *Son-Rise* the Kaufmans mention that there was some improvement for Raun through eliminating from his diet foods with artificial additives — which at least suggests that an inborn error of metabolism may be involved, perhaps affecting the auditory centers of the brain — and they, like others, were able to achieve successful results with behavior training and sensory stimulation. Similar programs on a broad front are actively being explored by the National Society for Autistic Children. Also, the development and availability of qualified day-care centers can greatly assist parents and their other children.

What we must remember is that developmental disabilities are *not* diseases and thus cannot be "caught" or "cured." They are disorders that can be more or less successfully remediated, though success may sometimes mean keeping the condition from getting worse as the child grows. Crucial to that end are efforts to relieve parents from having to assemble the full picture and prepare a plan in the face of uncertainty about what they have never before encountered. I personally feel that a great deal of time and money could be saved, to the immense satisfaction of *all*, if information were coordinated through a qualified physician or social worker concerned the full spectrum of case management and capable of making viable recommendations.

I also believe that we would realize many opportunities now lost if the various organizations and services, both public and private, were to concert their efforts to a greater degree, improving communications about separate aspects of brain handicap so that we could begin to understand their interrelation. The merger of private organizations alone, into a single Brain Society, would make the largest nonprofit agency in the world, one capable of setting workable priorities, unifying research and creating model services.

In assisting *any* child to full and whole development, we should bear in mind the basic human rights that each youngster is entitled to:

> The Right to caring parents
> The Right to food, shelter and clothing
> The Right to be secure at home
> The Right to treatment
> The Right to get about in the community
> The Right to try and learn
> The Right to fair punishment
> The Right to understandable answers
> The Right to equal services and opportunities
> The Right to advocacy under law
> The Right to be listened to
> The Right to help and be helped
> The Right to the dignity of risk.

We *all* have a vested interest in the well-being of *every* child, so that development fulfills individual potentials, enhanced by meaningful education, health care and home environment, and entry into adult society is a welcome event, not the traumatic experience common today. But as many of us are aware, we seem to have become somewhat preoccupied with the outer space of the universe while remaining backward about the inner space of the mind.

The pursuit of self-interest in society at large must soon give way as the chief measure of human endeavor — starting at the top with leadership — and there are very real advantages to uniting in an effort to ensure the quality, rather than the quantity, of life. Such an effort begins with the understanding that a healthy brain is focal to each person and, in turn, all people: that if we demean others, we demean our *own* humanity.

To cite several advantages, money should be lowest on the scale but, as an old Hindu proverb goes, "Mention cash and raise the dead." The direct cost of *not* uniting on brain handicap is much greater, as measured by duplication, than a concerted effort. Additionally, the piecemeal approach has a higher rate of failure, leading to institutional treatment for a minimum cost of $12,000 (and rising) per patient annually, not counting millions in capital outlay for each facility. Where they succeed, disparate services may achieve little more than a mediocre outcome. However, there are many indirect costs as well: unresolved problems in the classroom, delinquency, sibling anxieties, lack of adequate training and ensuing taxpaid unemployment, neglect of basic health care until it becomes an expensive health crisis, family disintegration.

Splintering knowledge is a classic way to retard research. There are of course good and valid reasons for specialization, but if each field conducts studies without adequately communicating with others, the pogo stick of progress tends to describe an erratic forward motion, and it is then discovered after the fact that what was thought to be an advance is actually a regression. Schools have gone rapidly into special education without fully evaluating the psychological impact of this type of segregation; what biochemists learn takes years to filter into practice; nutritional therapy is resisted as a fad by certain drug therapists. Even within professions, there seem to be disparities arising from various conventions, methods accepted in one region being rejected in another. And reference material becomes so compartmentalized and voluminous that often the whole cannot be seen for the sum of its parts.

But the main advantage, apart from money and research, of integrating efforts to ameliorate brain handicap is the savings in human anguish. Each year, every year, many children continue to sustain brain impairment and need our help in minimizing the disability. The fact that it can grow worse through delayed care is linked to problems of coordination in using existing knowledge. We may speak of the afflicted child and the deprivation that child faces in trying to manage in an increasingly complex world. But, equally important, we must recognize that the direct measure of service deficits is the heavy burden placed upon parents and their other children. They, too, struggle with uncertainties and social problems; for anxiety over any chronic illness is always greatly magnified — to the point of almost becoming a disease in itself. This could be avoided or greatly relieved, to the benefit of communities everywhere, if those in the field came together instead of following exclusive courses, if we all worked *on* the mind instead of giving each other an occasional piece of it.

We need to cooperate as a team — parents, professionals and volunteers alike — not as isolated entities obliged to handle one another. For each of us has sustained lasting wounds from untoward experience during development. Extremes may be apparent, but the shadings in between are often slight, which brings major focus to the ways in which we cope — important to someone who has been labeled or rejected at an early age, but also just as important to everyone.

The primary aspect of such a team must be the family — for several reasons. First, parents are the ones directly on the scene every day, capable of observing and responding to the full range of consequences of brain handicap. This is *their* child, *their* home, *their* family, *their* resources, and it is through *their* efforts that the child is seen by others. They *must* know what to do and be given a program to follow. Otherwise, they are in the position of being on the front line, unarmed, without a plan, and no map.

Second, in the interests of the child and the home environment upon which effective treatment depends, professional authority has to be flexible enough to allow parents to coordinate efforts through a social worker or family doctor in order to avoid situations in which separate instructions may be in conflict or lack bearing on actual needs. At the least, questions from parents should be openly welcomed and openly answered.

Third, help from schools usually does not begin until age five, but it is during the child's first two or three years that early intervention and emotional support count most. There is a great deal that an informed, partisan and loving family can do for *any* child, and this applies especially to the child with a developmental disability. As M. A. Hofer of the Albert Einstein College of Medicine states in his introduction to the Ciba Foundation Symposium, *Parent-Infant Interaction*: "Over the past decade, we have come to recognize that the early parent-infant relationship has a profound impact on the development of emotional behavior, cognitive faculties, even biological organization and resistance to illness."

In short, our understanding of brain function and child development will mean a better world by improving the way we perceive and interact with one another, recognizing that what we *believe* conditions what we *do*. For the warm, accepting society can solve most problems, sooner or later, while the hostile, unaccepting society creates more problems than it ever resolves.

◼ Prevention

ACCORDING TO THE CALIFORNIA ASSOCIATION FOR the Retarded, every five minutes another mentally handicapped child is born in the United States. Some of these children suffer from pregnancy disorders, some from genetic changes, some from birth accidents. More are subsequently harmed by errors in early care, infections, head injury, malnutrition and environmental stress. Seriously underfed children are especially at risk. Around five million in our public schools, or one in every classroom, manifest the minimal brain dysfunction of hyperactivity and other learning problems.

The President's Committee on Mental Retardation, as well as the National Association for Retarded Citizens, estimates that fifty percent of this incidence is preventable. Surely that estimate can someday be raised, for many pregnancy disorders, inherited difficulties and birth accidents are now avoidable; and *no* child need suffer bad care, untreated infections and injury, hunger or destructive pressures. Eventual total prevention is obviously an unrealistic dream, but where optimum development of children is concerned, we should always set our sights high.

To qualify this view without causing undue anxiety, let us take the extremely rare case of a little girl we'll call Babs, youngest of three happy, healthy children. Her father earned a good living as an engineer; her mother was an excellent homemaker. There were no complications during pregnancy or at birth. Babs was a delightful baby. Coincidentally, before she was born, the family had been moved to a Midwestern state, where environmental iodine levels were low, and neither mother nor child was given a thyroid test (which is not yet routine and in any event could be omitted because earlier pregnancies had gone well). By the time it was noted that Babs's physical and mental growth seemed stunted, it was too late: she was severely retarded because of a deficiency of thyroid hormone.

Through no one's "fault," the family was nonetheless confronted with major annual expenses, some of which were borne by state and federal programs. They also faced the heartbreak of knowing that Babs would never lead a productive life. This personal tragedy cost society a contributor, so the total levy must include *both* the resulting care *and* the loss of a taxpayer, or around $15,000 a year for a minimum of fifty years — three quarters of a million dollars as opposed to a few dollars for one thyroid test and treatment with thyroxin.

We are not talking about the need for spectacular scientific breakthroughs to achieve prevention but the need to take nothing for granted in applying knowledge that has been in existence for years, to err prudently on the side of caution. Multiplying the basic annual cost by three percent of the population, the national burden on individuals, communities, counties, states and the federal government comes to at least $90 billion, with the actual figure probably being much higher. Comparatively, the exercise of known means of prevention would cost about one percent of that, or $900 million — maybe less if handled by a system of clinics, paid for by the interest from one deposit of $20 billion, the private in-trust investment of which would also stimulate the economy, as would the resulting tax relief.

Clearly, there could be great hope for all in such a program, if we established positive courses of action and reordered our goals to give preventive measures equal standing with courses of treatment after something has happened. Meanwhile, each family can do much on its own to ensure safe child development through awareness of the causes of brain handicap and how to avoid them, concurrently improving the evolution of every youngster.

Since prevention of developmental disabilities is a large subject, an accurate grasp of it entails as comprehensive an approach as possible, at the risk of overlap in reviewing both the contributory and specific factors involved, along with trying to detail the ways in which they interface. Therefore, it is crucial to understand some of the general considerations first as a preface to discussing the many identified particulars.

Anoxia is a critically low level of oxygen in the bloodstream. In the main, it occurs whenever breathing is interrupted for a prolonged period, or when the heart stops beating for more than four minutes. This can happen at birth, as well as following injuries or strokes in later years. The tissue most vulnerable to oxygen deprivation is the central nervous system, which uses only ten percent of the body's energy but requires twenty-five percent of its oxygen. Impairment of any part of the brain, at any time in life, is serious. When it happens during the child's developmental years, there is risk of pronounced mental disability; when it happens at birth, retardation is almost inevitable without proper care, severity being proportional to the degree of oxygen loss. While anoxia before birth may have other causes, anoxia at birth arises if the time between separation of the placenta from the wall of the uterus and the baby's first breath exceeds around ten minutes. So the importance of someone skilled in perinatal care cannot be overestimated as nature's alert agent to help all go well, particularly in cases of overly protracted labor.

Infections are another cause of brain injury. High childhood fevers can precipitate seizures, when body temperature exceeds neural tolerance levels. Even more critical are untreated illnesses of the mother during pregnancy. Any form of venereal disease has to be regarded as a threat to her reproductive system and the unborn child. Certain vaginal viruses, which all women contract, may cause fetal damage if they enter the cervix during the first three months of pregnancy, as the baby's brain is becoming organized. Similarly, if the mother comes down with rubella (German measles) during the first trimester, there is an increased chance of the child's being born mentally retarded. Women can now get a blood test to determine immunity and obtain pre-pregnancy shots if necessary. But in 1963-1964, an epidemic of German measles caused 30,000 miscarriages and 20,000 severely disabled babies, whose care has already cost the nation $2 billion, according to Congressman Paul G. Rogers (D-Fla.).

Head injury is a direct hazard that should never be taken lightly. Adults have developed epilepsy following accidents, fights and participation in contact sports, but the consequences of brain trauma are far more serious during childhood. Every year, 200,000 American youngsters are hospitalized for head injury, usually from automobile and bicycle accidents. Twenty thousand sustain permanent damage. The most frequently involved are between the ages of three and seven (*Chronic Illness in Children*), suggesting the need for improved safety, both on the street and in the car. Even a child's entry into the world can place stress on the brain if the head is unduly misshapen by contractions or the baby emerges face or feet first. It may be speculative to relate the insular quality of adult life to the rows of little isolation cells in a nursery, or an aggressive society to untender handling of new life, but it is no speculation at all to state flatly that indifferent treatment of the head at birth is dangerous to the brain. So are any head blows during the child's growing years.

Two other significant factors are diet and drugs. The effect of thalidomide on the unborn is an already documented tragedy. However, there are many drugs, licit and illicit, harmful to the fetus. Legal drugs include nonprescription items such as caffeine, nicotine and alcohol, as well as prescription pills like amphetamines and salt diuretics given to hold down the weight of pregnant women. Socially, the practice is ingrained to take something to wake up, to get through the day, to calm the nerves, to settle the stomach, to go to sleep. We often jest about having pills for all ills, but we also seem to have them for personal problems and coping with simple discomfort. The tremors and stiffness of parkinsonism, a nerve disease, can follow overuse of tranquilizers, according to Dr. I. S. Cooper, who pioneered the brain pacemaker. Dr. J. Robert Willson, of the University of Michigan Medical School, has found that certain sedatives, routinely and heavily prescribed, may produce mental retardation in infants. And Dr. Myron Winick notes in *Malnutrition and Brain Development* that drug-induced folic acid deficiency may result in congenital malformations.

Of course, everything ingested has relative values for the individual, both positive and negative. Since these vary from person to person, potential problems lie not so much in use as in abuse. When a woman is pregnant, she has another life inside her that is entirely dependent upon what she takes into her system. No one would give a cigarette or a cocktail to a baby, yet that is what happens to a certain extent when the mother smokes or drinks, alcohol and nicotine in her bloodstream circulating to the fetus, measurable by changes in its heartbeat. Only *unwise* intake is in question. Occasional moderate use may be both desirable and pleasurable. But if heavy drinking is unhealthy for the expectant mother, it is far more so for her unborn child: research at the University of Washington Medical School indicates that thirty to fifty percent of babies born to alcoholic mothers display an abnormality termed the fetal alcohol syndrome.

As for diet, mental retardation of severely under-nourished people is an observable fact, widely documented by many authorities. Myron Winick and others note that the same occurs in the womb if nutrients in the mother's bloodstream are not sufficient for proper growth; a poor maternal diet during pregnancy is thus related to impaired fetal development and a reduction in the number of brain cells. While malnutrition and low folic acid make poor women prone to underweight births (increasing the chances of mental disabilities and costing an estimated $5,000 per pound added to these dangerously small babies), even well-to-do women may be at risk through using a low-calorie, low-salt diet and salt diuretics — or so reports pregnancy nutritionist Dr. Tom Brewer to the Prevention Project of California's Association for the Retarded. In general, Dr. Brewer suggests that fear of weight gain during pregnancy is a learned fear, which can be corrected through a better understanding of proper nutrition.

There are also family eating patterns passed from one generation to another that can be harmful to the unborn. In some backwoods communities we've visited, the patterns are shared to the extent that it is difficult to tell who is retarded and who isn't because of anemia from overuse of starch. The propensity to ascribe such circumstances to inbreeding is simplistic, for time and again improvements may be realized through family dietary counsel, or when the children are placed in better-fed environments.

29

But the more widespread form of poor nutrition arises from our overreliance on speed meals and sugared snacks. No sound diet can be prepared in a flash, yet an entire generation has been raised on "instant foods." Fortunately, many people are now becoming aware of the basic food groups and the importance of planning a diet around them. This usually leaves little interest in or appetite for items that provide only calories, with insufficient proteins, minerals, fibers and vitamins. As respected professionals have increasingly guided the consumer, the market has responded to public concern and made great progress in recent years.

There are numerous other causes of brain handicap — tumors, pernicious anemia, emotional stress, metabolic errors, certain metal compounds and chemical poisons. Some may penetrate the chromosomes and be transmitted by them, but the vast majority are environmental, not genetic, and little is known about the biochemical basis of gene alteration.

An established measure of mental retardation continues to be the IQ test. A score of 1-29 is called severe, 30-50 trainable, and 51-70 educable. However, IQ can be raised through good nutrition and remedial activities, as demonstrated at St. Jude's Hospital of Memphis. What the tests do is check some aspects of some socially acceptable performance. If bears put on horn-rimmed glasses and gave IQ tests, we'd all flunk tree-climbing and hibernation and score retarded on back-scratching. Intelligence, on the other hand — which is not to be construed as having much to do with IQ — is genetic to the extent that size and shape of the brain at birth are inherited, while performance and use are learned, beginning with the rapid growth of refinements immediately after birth. Yet even in the transmission of intelligence from parent to child, many cultural factors are involved. If eating patterns have an impact, so do working, living and recreational patterns, and responses to emotional or unexpected situations. The mind, like the body, is adaptable. A child raised in a fearful environment is certainly going to have his perceptions altered by it. And a child entertained solely by television is going to develop a different consciousness and mental attitude than a child entertained by creative indoor and outdoor play.

It is through understanding these contributory factors that we can begin to use existing knowledge effectively to achieve prevention *now*, not in the future. Since the quality of life after birth is related to the quality of life before birth, there is no substitute for parental security and stability as a preface to childbearing. A happy home almost certainly has a prenatal influence on the fetus. This is not to say that parents need be endowed with material abundance: possessions and security are not the same thing. Rather it is to say that the climate between mother and father is best if free of anxiety. Real love has a potent way of making life glad. But when the mother is tense, the unborn child may be aware of her body tightening, just as a surge from her adrenal glands enters its bloodstream. Anytime stress is unrelieved or severe, there is greater probability of risk to the fetus. Perhaps the most constructive parental attitude is one that views having a baby as a twenty-five-year commitment to new life, beginning with ensuring the health and happiness of the home during pregnancy — a perspective from which both mother and father see the ways to help each other.

Within the perimeter of parental security, further measures basic to prevention have a better chance of being recognized and used. High on the list is good pre-, peri- and postnatal care. Yet it's estimated by the National Center for Health Statistics that around thirty percent of expectant mothers do not seek such medical attention, and that nearly forty-four percent of births are unplanned. Every pregnant woman, whether or not she can afford it, should be entitled to the services of an obstetrics clinic. And every parent owes it to self, spouse and child to be familiar with at least a few of the many excellent books on childbirth now available.

Of late, there has been growing interest in having babies born at home rather than in a hospital. While this may allow a highly satisfactory experience in many uncomplicated situations, speeding parent-infant interaction, it does pose risks to mother and baby if there are exceptional circumstances. Even if they don't occur, there are a variety of things, before and after birth, instrumental to preventing a developmental disability that cannot be performed in the bedroom, such as PKU and blood tests, high-risk screening, and special assistance in the event of anoxia.

For all parents, with or without medical care during pregnancy, it is imperative that the expectant mother have safe exercise, proper nutrition, good hygiene and no intake of drugs unless necessary. Safe exercise consists of practically any activity — in addition to helpful routines prescribed by obstetricians — that does not injure the fetus or exhaust the mother and not only maintains physical condition for the labor of birth but also helps improve circulation. In turn, a healthy mother tends to sleep better at night and so is less apt to feel tired during the day.

Proper nutrition forms the basis of food reaching the baby and depends upon a balanced diet, essential to growth, that keeps up the mother's stamina, too. When intake is spaced frequently throughout the day in small amounts, blood sugar levels remain more even, overweight from junk foods is avoided, and there is less chance of having to take medication to relieve morning sickness. In general, the better the diet, the easier the delivery, the healthier both mother and child.

Good hygiene is the first line of protection against infection. This, of course, applies to the father as well as the mother. A sick mother's energies are drained, and if the illness is chronic, her system may be sufficiently depleted to affect the well-being of her child.

As noted, overreliance on drugs seems to be a phenomenon of our times. The addictive use of any drug poses a threat, direct or potential, to the baby, and no woman should consider getting pregnant if she has a dependency. Similarly, the use of legal drugs, both prescription and nonprescription, should be regarded with caution. Heavy smoking during pregnancy is now recognized as being implicated in reducing the baby's size; too much coffee may stimulate fetal restlessness during required periods of quiescence; and excessive use of aspirin can be harmful. If the home is happy and the mother healthy, that is the best medicine.

Since the extent of brain damage is related to the stage of development at which it occurs — the earlier, the more profound — prevention has two key aspects: (1) preventing the disability before, at or soon after birth, and (2) preventing deterioration to improve chances for a whole and full life. This chapter deals primarily with the first. The rest of the book is devoted to the second.

As a basic preparation for healthy pregnancy, every woman should check her immunization against contagious diseases for which vaccines exist and are indicated. Despite the fact that German measles during the first trimester is a recognized hazard, there are no mandatory national programs for immunization. If a woman contracts rubella when she is pregnant, she faces the choice of either having an abortion or possibly bearing a severely handicapped child. Of course, recommendation for an abortion depends upon her having a doctor and the doctor being informed of the illness. Yet many women don't see an obstetrician until after the third month; others don't go until it is too late for safety, or when abortion would be legally problematical. How ironic that we have laws about taking life but no law to prevent impaired life through the simple act of immunization!

Although a serological test is usually required (as is a rubella test in states like California) prior to the formation of a legal marriage to determine if one partner or the other has syphilis, there is no way of applying it to those who simply cohabit. Syphilis, which can be a devastating legacy to the newborn child, is again on the rise. Since its detection is a simple medical procedure, those who would like to have a baby, under whatever circumstances, should be encouraged to have a blood test first when in doubt.

With most authorities in state and national agencies agreed that an estimated fifteen percent of developmental disabilities have some basis in genetic mutation, the field of cytogenetics has growing importance in terms of identifying high-risk couples before, or at least early into, a pregnancy. People who know that they have a strong chance of giving birth to a disabled child may wish to elect the alternate of adoption — *if* they are informed through genetic counseling. Yet both information and programs are not fully enough advanced.

Tay-Sachs disease, for instance, causes mental retardation and is eventually fatal, according to Dr. Richard Koch of Children's Hospital in Los Angeles. The infant is unable to use certain fatty substances in food. These accumulate in the brain, progressively destroying it. The carrier state of the disease, which strikes children of Eastern European Jewish background, can be identified. However, expectant parents often don't know the risks or haven't been advised about screening methods.

The technique of amniocentesis, in which a small amount of fluid is extracted from the fetal sac, can detect chromosomal abnormalities such as Down's syndrome (mongolism), damage from rubella, and spina bifida, an open lesion at the base of the spine that may result in paralysis and mental retardation. Until the substitute of a single blood test is developed, the procedure should be employed where indicated. But again, parents have to know to ask about it.

Recently, another promising advance in prenatal diagnosis has been developed by two Yale physicians, John C. Hobbins and Maurice J. Mahoney. Called fetoscopy, the technique makes possible for the first time direct visualization of the fetus. Although used now to diagnose inherited diseases of the blood, it has the potential of detecting some fetal structures which might indicate brain problems. The limitation here is that this technique is experimental and still under review.

Phenylketonuria, or PKU, is due to faulty metabolism of phenylalanine, an amino acid, in the newborn and causes irreversible infant retardation unless treated early. A simple blood test at birth reveals the condition, and a phenylalanine-restricted diet corrects it. Yet in out-of-hospital births this vital aspect of perinatal care cannot be applied unless the mother knowledgeably takes the initiative to obtain the test.

In galactosemia, an enzyme needed to convert galactose to glucose is missing in the infant; this results in retardation. Use of a diet low in galactose prevents brain damage, but screening for this deficiency remains largely neglected in postnatal care.

There are numerous biochemical imbalances, either naturally or artificially induced, that pose a hazard to the fetal brain — imbalances that can be checked, yet too often aren't. The artificial ones include a whole spectrum related to drug intake and excessive use of junk foods.

So it is helpful for the doctor to review the individual life-style and environment of the pregnant woman, in addition to examining her, and establish sound prenatal recommendations. Among the natural hazards are both dieting and overeating. Indeed, overeating may often be followed by crash dieting. The extreme weight gain of metabolic toxemia is characterized by high blood pressure, albumin in the urine and retention of fluid. It can be controlled by strict adherence to a special program, and *must* be controlled to avoid fetal brain damage. But severe dieting, on the other hand, can lead to the potentially harmful breakdown of fat products known as ketosis. Thus the ultimate concern in prenatal care is not arbitrarily holding weight to some ideal level. Rather, it involves consideration of what is most natural, healthy and comfortable for the individual mother, with careful attention to metabolic disorders that may accompany the pregnancy of even the most conscientious woman.

Still another cause of brain handicap is aging of the ovum. A man keeps producing sperm (whose quality depends upon his good health), but every female is born with a fixed set of ova. At puberty, these are released during ovulation once a month until menopause. On average, a woman has about forty years of fertility. However, the peak years are from the late teens to the mid-thirties, or roughly twenty years. The older the ovum, the greater the chance that it may become altered. While many women do bear healthy children during late middle age, there is a pronounced rise in the incidence of developmentally disabled babies born to those over the age of thirty-seven. This suggests at least a statistical advantage to earlier pregnancies and the need for sage professional advice when they occur in later years. Since the decision to have a child is both important and intensely personal, there are no set rules apart from the caring exercise of prudence. The begetting of life is *never* a risk-free process at *any* age.

Although child abuse may be considered by some to be a relatively rare cause of brain injury, in view of social progress made over Victorian concepts of child-raising, the incidence has become of increasing concern to authorities. Every year, around 60,000 cases are reported in the United States, with children so battered as to risk developmental disabilities. How many may go unreported is, of course, impossible to determine, though physicians such as Vincent J. Fontana, head of New York City's Task Force on Child Abuse, suggest that the number appears to be rising, with the heaviest concentration of fatalities occurring in the newborn-to-one-year age group. Incidents follow no social or economic lines. *Any* family under profound stress can be vulnerable, particularly if the parents themselves sustained harsh treatment during their own early years. No simple answers exist to this complicated problem, but responding to circumstances after the fact is in general less effective than understanding causes and endeavoring to remedy them. So in addition to day nurseries, no-questions-asked respite care services, early-alert programs and counseling, prevention could well involve an educational process to teach *and* prepare youth for the major responsibilities of parenting before they become parents. My own view, which I believe to be widely shared by educators and physicians, is that youngsters raised in an environment of neglect need help in unlearning the patterns of neglect, both through exposure to love and through kind instruction. This in turn would benefit children of secure and informed parents by reaffirming in class the scope of care underlying the honored privilege of being mother and father.

Focal attention should at all times be given to new parents, especially to the expectant mother; for the reality of bearing a first child is a most signal experience, physically and emotionally. Among the practical aspects, many pregnant young women may be bothered by irregularity and feel concerned that good health means moving one's bowels daily. Some laxatives offer relief only to create a dependency, but mineral oil — used by the poor because it is cheap — absorbs the fat-soluble vitamins, A, D, E and K, and a deficiency in these, if serious or prolonged, may harm the fetus and may, as well, possibly create compensatory overeating by the mother. Far better to follow a naturally laxative diet — dried and fresh fruit, bulk-producing grains and vegetables — with increased fluids.

Another potential difficulty in a first pregnancy is adjusting to a necessary change in life-style. Mentally accepting this from the start is important to the quality of acceptance for the baby. Research by Dr. Solco Tromp of the Netherlands suggests that extreme heat or dehydration during the first trimester can affect formation of the fetal brain, so if pregnancy ensues in very hot weather, and the expectant new mother enjoys strenuous activities, she should take special care to avoid fluid depletion. Or, as indicated, if she's been accustomed to excessive smoking and doesn't cut back (or better yet, quit smoking entirely), there is a greater chance that her child will have a low birth weight. In every such instance that may affect the natural course of fetal development, there is obviously a certain element of risk. Simple counseling from the start would go a long way toward ensuring a safe and happy term.

One common discomfort of first pregnancies is morning sickness, which on occasion may contribute to fluid depletion. However, this can often be relieved by a good balance of normal food intake, more frequently spaced and accompanied by daily B vitamins including B_6, pyridoxine. The need for B_6 in particular increases after conception because of fetal demand, and deficiency in it is thought by some investigators to be involved with mental retardation, pyridoxine being necessary for growth and the metabolism of amino acids, the building blocks of all proteins. As reported to the International Brain Research Organization by Dr. Storm van Leeuwen of the Netherlands, errors in metabolism may affect the central nervous system, with an observed relationship existing between B_6 in the blood and changes in brain waves.

Numerous biochemical imbalances in the mother can now be detected and corrected before problems arise. Testing thyroid levels is only one example. The routine check for diabetes is another. However, one test required in California but not nationally is for Rh-factor incompatibility in the parents. The factor, discovered in 1940, is an inheritable blood component found in eighty-five percent of the population. Those who have it are called Rh-positive, those who don't, Rh-negative. If a pregnant woman is Rh-negative, and the fetus is Rh-positive through inheritance from the father, blood passing into her system from the placenta stimulates the formation of antibodies, potentially fatal to her, potentially brain-damaging to the child. It is standard obstetrical practice to check the Rh factor of both parents — *if* the mother sees a doctor, *and* the father is available. But we have no requirement that an expectant mother must see a doctor, let alone submit to the test; sometimes the father may be absent or in doubt; and with home births, the check is made only if both parents take the initiative, knowingly, to go into a clinic.

Beriberi is a disease of malnutrition caused by an unbalanced diet low in vitamin B_1, thiamine. If untreated with B_1, the disease affects the nervous system, in particular the fetal brain. Fortunately, many foods now have B vitamins added. But for families that either omit or cannot afford these foods, one possibly inexpensive response might be to add brewer's yeast and wheat germ to the diet. Also helpful is a product called Yeast-Plus: a tablespoon stirred into the daily glass of orange juice. The B vitamins — essential to the use of carbohydrates, according to Dr. Lendon H. Smith of the University of Oregon Medical School — are synergistic, meaning they interact with one another. Research has yet to isolate the full complex, but they all occur naturally, in balance, in these low-cost foods.

Pellagra is also a nutritional disease found among those who overrely on diets lacking in niacin, another B vitamin. Having caused the deaths of thousands of Americans earlier in the century, pellagra has been thoroughly studied, and the poor are often found to be the ones who suffer. In its advanced stages, the disease is marked by skin lesions, gastrointestinal distress and psychosis; but by then, damage to the unborn child may already have occurred, so prevention calls for noting and correcting niacin deficiency *before* the physical signs appear.

Much the same can apply to pregnant women on a vegetarian diet — increasingly popular in the United States. Here the principal nutrient missing is vitamin B_{12}, which is needed for the development of red blood cells, nerve tissue and the brain. Again, potential problems can be avoided through adding the proper supplements, if the expectant mother is aware that traditional vegetarian intake, as practiced in India, has to be *most* comprehensive.

In general, we must at all times remember that two of the major causes of disease are infection and poor nutrition. Poor nutrition also lowers resistance to infection and slows recovery. It is already implicated in mental retardation. Yet as Dr. Myron Winick suggests, medical education has largely ignored this.

A white-cell count taken at the start of a pregnancy assists in detecting latent infections and a red-cell count in determining incipient anemia, involved in one out of five neonatal situations, according to Dr. Peter Dallman, pediatrician at the University of California Medical School. While women who are carriers of such diseases as hepatitis may themselves not be ill, systemic impairment jeopardizes the formation of a healthy baby. In fact, the motor center damage of dystonia can follow acute meningitis; and studies of one hundred children hospitalized with the disease in London, as reported by Derek Richter to the International Brain Research Organization, showed a higher than normal rate of subsequent behavior problems.

Handling of the child at birth has now greatly improved in many hospitals, where the newborn is gently treated and kept by the mothers' side. The practice of allowing fathers to participate in deliveries, an offshoot of the pioneering work in natural childbirth done by Dr. Grantly Dick-Read of England, may have contributed to beneficial changes in procedure, enhancing the father's sense of being a part of things. And today, impressive work by obstetricians like Frederick Leboyer has successfully reduced trauma to the new infant. Moreover, rooming-in is now more available on a flexible basis. This allows the baby to be at all times with the mother, or to be taken to the nursery only during sleep, according to the mother's individual desires rather than prescribed routine. She is also often allowed to go home when ready instead of being held for a set number of days. In some hospitals, the minimum hold time permits her to leave the day of delivery, if she wishes and there are no complications. The importance of making known such personal preferences at birth is that it increases the parents' sense of participation and the quality of their interaction with the child.

While the influence of anoxia at birth has been discussed, an earlier form of it during pregnancy can arise from undue stress. If it is severe, the fetal brain may be affected. Anxiety knows no social class, but it has special import in poverty situations. Poverty mothers are prone to high-risk births on the one hand and, on the other, often lack adequate birth control. Caught between marginal means and the inevitability of another mouth to feed, these women experience a feeling of helplessness that has a bearing on the amount of oxygen their systems can supply. Should they then have developmentally disabled babies, their plight is further compounded. In looking to prevention, we need to attack the sources and causes of poverty, beginning with the cardinal right of every couple: the right *not* to have more children than are wanted, and to be helped toward that end if necessary. For according to data in *Contraceptive Technology*, serious perinatal hazards increase after the fourth birth, the incidence of gastrointestinal infections rises with family size, and children in large families tend to be physically smaller and lower in IQ than children from small families.

No wonder so many of us are committed to modifying inflexible religious opposition to birth control and abortion. The moral arguments against preventing life are based on many commendable pro-life beliefs, but an ambiguity does exist in terms. If abortion is deemed murder, then isn't miscarriage manslaughter, crib death suicide, damage to the fetus mutilation? Sixty percent of miscarried fetuses are flawed — God-created nature's way of aborting her mistakes. Should not people also have the option of aborting their mistakes? and doing it legally instead of illegally, as they did at the

44

rate of one million a year before laws were liberalized? If the rhythm method is morally acceptable, then what, really, is so immoral about other methods of contraception, including abortion when contraception has failed? Abortion is such a personal issue that it truly boils down more to the individual mother's feeling about it than to something that can be covered by rules. Also, pro-life views have to include greater consideration of the quality of life, both present and future, and to what extent it can be maintained if people have more children than they can properly care for. In the past five years, states Dr. Myron Winick in *Malnutrition and Brain Development*, we have come to realize "that malnutrition, a disease thought alien to the United States, is a significant problem in a large segment of our population." Worldwide, half a billion people already suffer acute hunger. Every week, ten thousand people in Asia, Africa and Latin America die of starvation. One hopes that our spiritual leaders will not only look upon but live with those dying in this slow, agonizing manner, and I pray that religious preoccupation with the privacy of the bedroom has not retarded our spiritual evolution of love.

In addition to being wanted, every child needs present and participating parents. Yet many demands often take parents away from home in an effort to secure and maintain it. Can there ever be real success or emancipation for anyone, unless from the moment of birth each knows the abiding love of mother and father, directly and meaningfully?

On a broader front, we must encourage agencies and services to move information from the policy level to the

45

operational level at a quicker pace. Right now, many great ideas have been advanced to further the well-being of evolving life, but most of them tend to remain on the shelf, since it's often easier to propose answers than to apply them. We know so much about how to prevent developmental disabilities. Our hope for the future now resides in trying to use what we know as a preface to improving upon it, so that every child may have the chance to develop as best as possible.

◙ Early Care

FOR PARENTS, THE REALIZATION THAT THEIR BABY may have a developmental disability is an almost invariably shattering experience. One *knows* that something does not seem well with the child — something hard to define because it is not an illness — yet at the same time one *hopes* that it is only temporary, that things will soon clear up. Since this uncertainty can be profoundly disturbing, full of mingled feelings under a seeming cloud of gloom, the first step is to put fear aside and accept the evident reality. Next is to think positively about what can be done, not about what can't, and start doing it.

Usually it is the mother who first senses a progressive difficulty in her child. Perhaps the baby manifests an odd listlessness, puzzling development, inability to suckle properly, or some other sign of deepening concern to her but accompanied by the very natural wish that it be a passing stage. When it is not, her first recourse is to the father, more for reassurance than for confirmation that she's right to be worried about something neither of them understands. At this point, further delay may occur, since *no one* can easily countenance the thought of brain handicap in a life only just begun, and seeking the prompt diagnostic assistance necessary can often feel like an admission of permanent defeat.

Every moment given over to such vacillation is a crucial moment lost, for it is in the first stages that parents have the best chance of preventing the disorder from becoming worse. Nothing is hopeless unless one abandons hope, and there is at least some hope at all stages of a developmental disability. But the greatest opportunity lies in effective early care. In fact, the principles involved, to the extent that they draw parents together, are those that would improve the growth of any youngster.

While responsibility for treatment is the physician's, many things of a nonmedical nature can be done at home. To appreciate these, it is important to keep in mind two facts: (1) that the intense period of development is from age zero to six, during which the child's brain trebles in size; and (2) that all information, of *any* sort, reaching the brain is sensory, and sensory only.

During the brain's rapid expansion, particularly in the first year when cell division is still continuing, healthy stimulation is of lasting significance. Consider a young plant. If a budding branch is pinched, it won't grow, though other branches can be helped to flourish, taking its place; if the main stalk is bent, the whole plant will be affected unless it is carefully straightened. Much the same applies to the young brain, only in a far more complex way, since the evolving organ consists of ten billion neurons surrounded by 100 billion glial cells. Each neuron also possesses millions of RNA (ribonucleic acid) molecules, 100,000 varieties of protein and develops up to 60,000 connections with other neurons.

The magnitude of those numbers, in a quart weighing only three pounds, is as difficult to conceptualize as the vastness of the universe, but suppose we took an adult brain and destroyed one neuron every minute of every day for 10,000 years. Half would still be left. On the other hand, if we harm the brain during infancy, the same effect could be accomplished in several months. So what is done at the start has staggering implications for the rest of life.

Negatively, this may underscore the seriousness of childhood brain handicap. Positively, it points to the immense potential of early intervention and continuing good care, not only to minimize the injury but to stimulate uninjured sections of the brain. For if one neuron, like a budding branch, is restricted, others can be helped to flourish in its stead, growth righted as far as possible by *encouraging* growth. The real limitations relate to the damage of neglect.

For various reasons, those specializing in child development have separated the first six years of life into three stages: from birth to walking, walking to age three, and age three to school. But to simplify, this chapter is directed to the initial eighteen months and the next chapter to the following period until age five, when formal education generally begins.

Whatever the pros and cons of educational assistance, society cannot be expected to replace parents, nor should parents take the attitude that the start of school implies more than a recess from parenting. *Any* child's constructive participation in class depends almost entirely upon what is done at home *before* he or she reaches school. So it is an understatement to say that every year of early loving care is worth ten thereafter.

In some families, love and attention are looked upon as expressions that will "spoil" a child by rewarding demands, thereby encouraging overly demanding behavior, emotional weakness and personality flaws. Under such a concept, the main elements of attention may become acts of disapproval, or forcing conformity instead of recognizing, responding to and appreciating the child's needs; love is held back, as a feeling to be acknowledged, not shown. In point of fact, however, open affection is the strongest possible aid to development, and physical contact is intrinsic to psychic survival in the very young. Children who *act* spoiled usually feel insecure — pampered publicly, denied privately — and have developed unsatisfactory ways of exacting from their environment the necessary attention refused them. Truly loved children, respected from birth as individuals, have a much better chance of thriving than others, for the climate of love in a happy home increases mental ability to absorb and respond, to grasp the relation between personal needs and the needs of others; while adult rigidity or remoteness, stemming from doubt and a failure to trust intuitions, only causes problems by obliging the youngster to adapt to everyone else, to learn internal isolation as a way of life.

As to the second fact — that all information reaching the brain is sensory — the word "information" is often regarded by adults as thought expressed verbally, in speech or writing. However, speech is a system of sounds that reaches the brain through the ear, just as writing is a sequence of visual symbols that reaches the brain through the eye. In addition to the sensory organs of eye and ear, the brain also acquires information about the world around through the senses of touch, taste, smell, movement and rhythm of internal organs. Each of these senses is capable of receiving highly complex signals. The eye not only differentiates between light and dark, it can determine shapes, colors, distance, opacity, transparency, mobility, stability, elevation and direction. Touch defines something rough, smooth, soft, hard, wet, dry, hot, cold, sharp, blunt, painful, tickling, caressing. Taste relays sweetness, sourness, saltiness, bitterness and all the many subtle admixtures of these elements, while the ear, nose and other sensors pick up an equally sophisticated range of things that, through the interpretation of experience, become associated into meanings that are then used to convey a variety of impressions, from hunger and discomfort to the abstract called thought.

Though we sometimes deny it, there may be a nonexternal sense, possibly associated with the subconscious ability to detect trace odors. This sense seems to be dampened as people grow older and are taught to mistrust what cannot be explained, but it is quite apparent in young children, who will suddenly have a feeling about someone or some place for no apparent reason; and in adults, there is the phenomenon known as extrasensory perception, hunches, "vibes." Whatever the exact number of senses we agree exists, each is processed first in the brain by a cluster of specialized neurons, or "center," which selects, relays and stores information. This is called learning. Degree and quality depend *entirely* upon the amount of sensory stimulation, with the growth of each center enhanced by use.

Repetition of a stimulus causes a change in consciousness. Utter a pet word over and over and it will presently seem altered, perhaps absurd. Listen to a drip from the faucet long enough and it becomes an irritation. Children exposed to one set of cultural repetitions have a different grasp of language and music than those exposed to another. If we repeat that conformity is desirable, nonconformity may appear objectionable yet at the same time gain interest by being forbidden. Or if a child frequently receives unfair discipline, consciousness of behavior includes the refined practice of deception or manipulation — as happens when someone is punished for expressing a need and learns the ways of meeting it furtively.

Sensory deprivation shortens retention. Complex experience lengthens it. Technically, as observed in various rat experiments, stimulation tends to increase cortical protein and enzyme activity, while isolation decreases both. Even for thoughts to progress from point A to point B, each of us requires some external stimuli. Following World War II, we learned that adults can be brainwashed by prolonged confinement in a small, dark cells — not so much because they agree with their captors but because they have little left with which to disagree. Indeed, the principal agony of solitary confinement in penal institutions is mental, a punishment resulting in subdued behavior. This effect may be more pronounced in small children denied variety in overly restrictive homes that lack sufficient sensory experiences for best growth of the young brain. When life becomes too much a matter of sameness, the developing personality can be rendered permanently somber.

There aren't just several *levels* of consciousness, there are several *types* of it. We are born with every evolutionary imprinting basic to survival. Each is expanded by use. And the types of awareness that emerge are connected in distinctly individual ways — center to center, lobe to lobe, hemisphere to hemisphere. These can be employed to improve the abilities of a brain-handicapped child if parents keep in mind that everything known comes through the senses, that with stimulation they can help their youngster learn to increase assets, reduce deficits.

No child runs without first sitting up, crawling, standing, toddling and walking. If there's a leg problem, we don't restrain but *show how to compensate*. By the same token, if there is a developmental disability, it's important not to limit sensory stimulation but to expand it — bearing in mind that *all* things learned, not just physical performance, progress at different rates for different people. A baby's attempt to respond with body motions forms the basis for future acquisition of speech; and smiling — unlike gas-pain grimacing — doesn't come naturally or on schedule after a few weeks of life. As reported by the Ciba Symposium, *Parent-Infant In-*

53

teraction, babies *learn* to smile in response to affection, remain somber in the absence of it.

When attentive parents first notice any adverse change in their infant, they need the assistance of a physician qualified to evaluate developmental lags. There is no fixed way to secure the best doctor for a given family, but by requesting references from friends, relatives and neighbors, parents can usually obtain — *and* stick with — an able professional who will steer them to the appropriate specialists and will be concerned with integrating diagnoses. Since the process of determining precisely what is the difficulty and how to proceed may seem complex, parents should not be afraid to ask hard questions of the doctor about what they don't understand. Nor should they be afraid to trust their own intuitions when reporting observations on the child's progress. But by the same token, if they persist in a spirit of cooperation, they can help improve the quality of doctor-patient communication so vital to the quest.

From the first, a health record, such as recommended by Dr. A. Frederick North, Jr., in *Infant Care*, should be maintained *by parents* in notebook form for each child, covering on separate pages: full identification and insurance, emergency information, immunizations, any hospital admissions, accidents, special tests, disease history, allergies, pronounced problems, physical examinations, acute illnesses, medications, development progress. This is helpful to the parents in remembering specific events and forms a document that accompanies the child should parents happen to move or change services. It is also an aid to the doctor in delivering alert, prompt and comprehensive care, as well as in obtaining the correct information for office files.

An important problem of brain handicap is reduced sensory experience. When a child has an epileptic episode, sensations may be blocked or altered for a while by unconsciousness; with retardation, the ability to receive and initiate adequate stimulation is lowered; with cerebral palsy, mobility is difficult; and with autism, there is a gap between the child and the outside world. Anything that restricts the brain during the years it is trebling in size will create a developmental lag because of impaired sensory reception. Moreover, these children often don't receive as much stimulation as others when they actually need *more* stimulation than normal for optimum growth. Place *any* baby in an insular environment for long periods and the healthy development of its brain will likely be impeded. Social deprivation during the first six months of life can occur when infants are not picked up and fondled sufficiently while awake. In short, *child care and brain development are intimately related*, and it is urgent that we dispense with the notion that they are not, that the quality of individual handling makes no difference. Each human is born with a formed but undeveloped brain. Growth and refinements begin at birth, and parents can help minimize brain handicap through a program of infant sensory stimulation, which also provides them with many welcome activities oriented around their baby.

The program involves use of touch, taste, movement, sound, smell, sight and play, by mother *and* father.

Basics are simple, within the natural means of most parents, but since tender loving care (TLC) is indispensable, we should first clarify the difference between what is meant by mother and a woman, father and a man. Culturally, the tendency is to assume that arrival at puberty makes a girl a woman and boy a man, that when the two reproduce, they automatically become mother and father. This is biologically correct. The larger meaning, however, has little to do with gonadal activity. Instead, maturity emanates from individual confidence, self-esteem and resultant responsibility — an internal area enabling the person to see life as more than a function of self-gratification, physical performance or private profit. Males and females remain boys and girls, regardless of age, until they arrive at recognition and acceptance of the concept, "I love you as I love myself." And they remain men and women, satisfying desires on a course of diminishing returns, until capable of "adopting" their child, in the full sense of the word, regardless of attributes, meaning, "We love you as we do ourselves and endorse you from the hour of your birth to the very last moments of our lives." Then, and then only, do they begin to understand the constantly unfolding, unpredictable voyage of discovery of being mother and father, able to help and share with each other in moments both large and small, without debating who is supposed to do what, with which and to whom. Sometimes mothers and fathers are born in the face of travail, not running away from adversity but confronting reality, trying to seek answers together. Essentially, then, a mother is a

56

woman, with or without a partner, who extends the strength of her maternal love to a child; and a father is a man who, under whatever personal circumstance, has found the ways of expressing paternal love. In that spirit, TLC follows naturally, and the program of infant sensory stimulation becomes a joy rather than a method, an exercise of care rather than a routine, a fulfillment rather than a practice.

In *Son-Rise*, Barry Kaufman tells how his wife, Suzi, had to take their four-week-old son, Raun, sick with an ear infection, in blankets to the doctor's office. Raun was ill enough to require emergency hospitalization in the intensive care unit. Although he recovered, the infection involved auditory impairment that, eleven months later, led to hearing insensitivity and, subsequently, the first signs of autism: fascination with inanimate objects, disconnected experience, ear and eye difficulties. After sharing their fears, the Kaufmans embarked upon a course of sensory stimulation that, many hard, dedicated weeks later, successfully reversed the child's condition.

Such a supportive climate is indispensable to the mental health of all children. It is of major importance during early years in overcoming a developmental disability to whatever extent possible. The best surrounding atmosphere is a nursery with minimal inclusion of items that don't involve parental participation. For nine months, the baby has been enveloped in the womb, then extruded by birth into separate but dependent life, and gadgetry just isn't a substitute for fondling. The only recourse a baby has to express a need is to cry, and its primary need, apart from food and comfort, is to feel human, not mechanical, reassurance in the absence of the womb.

Any nursery should be both simple and inviting — warm, clean, cheerful, safe, close enough to where parents sleep so they can hear the cry for them. If relaxed surroundings are good for the baby, they're just as good for the parents, whose sense of ease and happiness contributes to the quality of handling. Rocking, for instance, is a form of early stimulation that activates kinesthesis, or muscular sensation of movement. The involuntary body response can be observed in a baby when it is raised and with gentle quickness lowered, producing a slight but visible tension in limbs and abdomen. Prior to birth, motion awareness is aroused in the fetus by the mother's activities as she walks, plays or exercises. After birth, the same is accomplished when the baby is rocked or carried. Done regularly, this continues the natural sensory experience of kinesthesis.

When loving parents handle, fondle, comfort, laugh and play with their baby, another type of stimulation is brought to bear, using sound and touch associated with pleasure. Before vision develops, everything reaching the brain comes primarily through these senses, as well as through the taste of nursing. The more this affection is given the better. Yet when something is seen to be not right with the new child, there can be an inclination to minimize such handling as being inappropriate or perhaps unsafe, and so the infant most in need is often denied instead of receiving extra effort. On occasion, too, a developmentally disabled baby may have reduced means of calling for or responding to physical reassurance, in turn making parents hesitate to extend it. Better to trust one's own native sense of love and to act accordingly, without worry.

Breast-feeding, once unfashionable, has fortunately been regaining respect in the past decade as both natural and good. Sucking on rubber or latex to ingest formula is only a substitute for drawing on the breast, sensing flesh to flesh while drinking mother's milk. It also deprives the mother of feelings associated with the profound intimacy of nursing. Women who wish to breast-feed successfully can obtain much helpful advice by contacting, early in pregnancy, La Leche League International, 9616 Minneapolis Avenue, Franklin Park, Illinois 60131. Established by a group of experienced mothers, the League has developed workable answers to a variety of potential problems that previously were thought to result in nursing failures. Of course, some women may be physically unable to breast-feed, and in such instances bottle-feeding is the only answer. But women who refuse to breast-feed because they find it repugnant, inconvenient or a threat to their figures should perhaps have faced that fact before getting pregnant. The mother's acceptance of a totally dependent life is crucial to its evolution — as well as good health from the protective properties of human milk. Additionally, lactation is known to reduce fertility, so the nursing mother has less chance of becoming pregnant again too soon for her baby's good. Only the mother can know the sense of having her breast drawn upon, and that sense is a two-way experience felt also by the baby. Everything felt by the baby is part of infant stimulation.

Although breast-feeding helps the uterus return to normal size, bottle-feeding should not be viewed as a case of either/or. It can be an interim convenience that allows the father to hold and feed the child, contributing to infant awareness that not just one but two parents are involved, and offering the father an opportunity to establish deep, early bonds with his baby. If the sensory act of caring for the infant from the beginning is marked by the mutual love of mother and father, they and their child have the best chance of continued sound development.

During the first weeks of life, the brain evolves through periods of waking, sleeping, feeding, bathing and being changed. These are explorations of the surrounding world, and their quality can be improved. Attention to the comfort of being changed has direct bearing on the baby's growing concepts of comfort. Too, the act of changing offers an opportunity to increase stimulation: wiping the baby clean, raising and lowering the legs and buttocks, patting on talc, applying the fresh diaper, nuzzling the stomach and neck, tickling the toes, touching the hands together, cooing, finally picking up and cuddling. Such activities are strong tactile and auditory experiences for the delicate newborn, and they are oriented around a realistic task, whose conclusion is accompanied by the pleasurable reward of a fresh diaper. This is what *all* infant stimulation is about: the use of senses by relaxed parents in the fulfillment of meaningful acts, which should be as prolonged as possible in the event of a developmental disability to accentuate what the absorbing mind receives.

Bath time again offers an opportunity to utilize a remarkable set of sensations. Most of the baby's body except the head — with the head back and supported by the left arm while the right hand does the washing (the other way around for lefties) — is immersed in water pleasantly warm to the touch, not only creating awareness of "warm" and "water" but reproducing outside the womb its fluid environment. There are the sounds of splashing, the gentle massage of being washed and dried, movement of arms and legs, the talk and laughter of parents. For the very first bath, however, a gradual approach, bringing hands and feet into contact with bath water, until the sense of water is identified, accepted and enjoyed, should preface immersion.

If pragmatic tasks have significance in early stimulation, so do the ways in which periods of general wakefulness are used. Soft singing, accompanied by rocking, activates and relates the brain's auditory and kinesthetic centers. In this relation reside the beginnings of nonpragmatic pleasures, or early concepts of entertainment. The same applies to games like shoe-the-old-horse and pat-a-cake. Since such games are among the first "abstract" mental activities, they help expand the baby's attention, a necessary prelude to the ability to grasp more complex associations. They are also a way of encouraging initiative response so that the emerging personality feels "I can do," not just what is done to him or her. After the baby's eyes begin to see and focus, visual stimulation continues the development of attention, through playing peek-a-boo. Since one aspect of retardation is a reduced attention span, this first sensory play can do much to increase consciousness.

The new brain, whatever its individual construct, is much like a blank slate upon which impressions are drawn. From the initial ones grow intricacies. Parents are thus engaged in creating a portrait of life, an artistry more amazing than the seven wonders of the world put together. If the lines are happy, they will reap joy, and as progress continues, the baby's physical condition will improve to the point where the elements of secondary stimulation can be used.

The first set of these secondary elements is gross-motor exercises, or improving tone in the large muscles of arms and legs — those required to sit up, crawl, stand and walk. With a developmental disability, gross-motor uses may be somewhat slow in coming along. Stimulation simply helps advance the process. The best setting is a comfortably warm room that permits little or no clothing, and a blanket spread on the floor. With the baby centered on the blanket, parents can employ a routine of six basic exercises: (1) raising, lowering and crossing its arms, one at a time and together, while the baby is on its back; (2) raising, lowering and crossing the legs, one at a time and together, also while the baby is on its back; (3) extending one leg at right angles to the body, touching it to the floor first on one side, then across to the other, repeating with the second leg; (4) with the baby still on its back, bending its knees up to the chest, separately and together; (5) with the baby on its stomach, raising both legs upward by the feet, gently arching the back; and (6) concluding with the game of reached-for objects.

All these exercises should be conducted in the spirit of play, not athletic training, and with close attention to stretching, not pushing, physical limits. In the event of cerebral palsy, or any orthopedic problem, they should *only* be used with the advice of a trained therapist.

The second set is visual and fine-motor exercises — eye-hand coordination. Here again, the routine employs a simple sequence of procedures: (1) light objects of varying density — a feather, soap bubbles, handkerchief or ball of yarn — are dropped on the baby from differing heights so that its eyes can follow and its hands respond; (2) the baby is given objects to feel, tactile shapes safe to hold and taste, one by one, then one in each hand; (3) overhead, bright colorful designs are moved up and down, back and forth, shifting after the baby's eyes focus on position or direction; (4) placing a block in each of the baby's hands, parents first bring the hands together so that the blocks clack; then the baby is encouraged to try the exercise independently; (5) with the baby held facing a mirror, it is then helped to touch the reflection with hand and mouth, identifying image and the visual impression of self-motion; and (6) the baby is given simple things to taste and smell to help stimulate recognition of these sensations — a sugar cube, lemon, raw carrot, peeled potato, mild onion — items that the baby can pick up and from which discover different flavors or odors. Of course, all should be large enough to prevent them from being accidentally swallowed.

Beyond such daily exercises, the secondary phase of

stimulation also includes a growing use of sounds and play. Each family, without having to spend much on sound-producing equipment, can manage to increase auditory sensations with a rattle, bell, clacking spoons, by singing, talking, laughing and clapping. But a music box, or radio playing soft music, adds to the dimension, and every compatible sound augments the capacity of the brain's auditory centers. As for games, a host of activities, beginning with the simple and increasing in complexity, are available in any home and serve to lengthen attention span. Rolling and retrieving a ball, stacking objects like blocks or pans, playing with colors, water, sand, tops, an inner tube, a large cardboard box and other simple things can be unending sources of fascination to the youngster.

Infant sensory stimulation is but an extension of the love of two caring people for their child. Most of it comes naturally to those who have confidence in each other. All of it is essential to early intervention with a developmental disability. We may live at a time when some parents are anxious about their feelings, and new parents persuaded that everything *but* their instincts count. Yet in the relaxed acceptance of oneself, whatever the ups or downs, lie the beginnings of full endorsement of another.

Sound nutrition is as important to the nursing mother as it is to the pregnant woman and should continue to consist as much as possible of wholesome foods. The quality of her milk depends upon a well-balanced diet. It also depends upon continued avoidance of unnecessary drugs. Proper intake helps maintain her good health and stamina until the child is weaned. Much the same applies to the mother who cannot nurse, her energies being just as indispensable to infant care and efforts to minimize a developmental disability.

Equal to the act of preparing nutritious food is finding the time to sit, eat and talk in an unstressful way. By planning ahead and using periods when the baby is asleep, parents usually find it possible to enjoy relaxed meals. Table talk affords both an opportunity to confer on the child's progress, exchange ideas and enhance the spirit of open communication necessary to their management of brain handicap. Here, the father can greatly assist by arranging to review menu and schedule, doing the grocery shopping on his way home from work or on weekends, and attending to some of the cooking or cleanup, to whatever extent his job allows. In short, close teamwork on all matters is very much at issue.

Some parents may have grandparents or relatives to help out during the first months. Others may wish to rely on each other only — perhaps hiring a high school girl for part-time housework. Whatever the individual preference, in the event of a developmental disability the father and mother must both work with doctor, social worker or public health nurse to ensure best progress at any given point and to prepare the basis for future selection of supplementary services.

It is also useful if both attend any examination of their child. Each needs to be directly informed and, through joint involvement, to extend emotional support to the other. There are many things that have to be checked out in an examination — blood tests, reflexes, motor development, head size and shape, sight, hearing, heart, lungs, and so on — and the doctor who has a way with infants can usually make the process relaxed. In particular, any sensory problem in a baby is serious unless compensated for promptly, and developmental lags should be confirmed by the appropriate tests, which compare individual growth and performance against established standards for given ages. Or if there are any feeding, digestive and allergic difficulties, the earlier corrective programs are initiated the better.

One sense sometimes overlooked is hearing when the baby is small. Even total deafness can go undetected, though it is simple enough to observe the presence or absence of a startle response to the snap of fingers, or the turning of the head to the ring of a tuning fork, *if* the infant has those abilities. But there are gradations of hearing problems, from limitations in sound range to dysfunction of the auditory centers, that are hard to diagnose until the child reaches speaking age. By then, much time has been lost. When parents suspect such a disability, they should seek a qualified specialist for early advice on what to do.

The labor of parenthood, leading to so many joys, may sound like a lot of work. It is. And couples should not bring a child into this world without expecting it. A whole and healthy baby requires years of care. That effort is magnified by the presence of a developmental disability. But when brain handicap cannot be avoided, swift efforts to intervene with infant sensory stimulation may reduce subsequent hardships, for parents and youngster alike.

The developmental needs of any human being at any age are love, a sense of belonging and a fruitful means of self-expression. Filling those needs takes work — showing affection, creating the climate of acceptance, teaching the ways to identify and use the variety of individual desires — and it begins with birth. Yet every adult also gains in self-fulfillment by having responsibility for a dependent life. Each of us is changed not only by receiving but by giving care. Existence itself has no more significant reward.

Development Record

Any professional working with developmental disabilities appreciates parents who keep an accurate record of their child's growth progress. The following sequence of dates, which is similar to that used by many agencies such as California's Regional Centers, is an aid to early detection of brain handicap.

Name_____ Date _____

Birth _____

Lifts head _____

Rolls over_____

Uses fingers _____

Smiles _____

67

Laughs _____

Sits _____

Crawls _____

Stands supported _____

Says "da" _____

Identifies name _____

Finger-feeds _____

Stands unsupported _____

Walks alone _____

Says first words _____

Spoon feeds _____

Uses cup _____

Combines words _____

Runs _____

Dresses _____

Toilet trained _____

Climbs steps alternating feet _____

Gives full name _____

▣ Later Detection

FROM WALKING AGE TO SCHOOL IS THE SECOND period of rapid brain growth. During it, signs of a developmental disability tend to appear more readily because of increased opportunity for social comparison. Not only do differences in children's performance levels become clearer, parents take pride in talking about them, especially when they may be prematurely attained. Sometimes youngsters are hurried into early achievement or coaxed to catch up if they don't seem to be coming along as fast as others. This can place untoward pressures on them when they may develop a lot one year only to be slowed the next and need most importantly to learn the basis of life: *acceptance of self for all its foibles*, not fear of being different or of failure to excel. Such social demands on formative preschoolers in turn condition the way they react to perceived weaknesses, and so they themselves often report an emerging limitation in one of their friends.

There are *average* times for children to acquire various skills; then there are the natural and desirable *individual* times. It may be *average* for a child to walk by the age of twelve or thirteen months, but some youngsters walk at nine months, others not until fifteen to eighteen months — a variance of over half a year, which is a substantial percentage of life to that point and does not reflect on intellect. The right time depends upon the child's readiness, not the clock or someone else's readiness.

For parents, it can of course be worrisome to see other children perhaps coming along a little faster than their own. Privately, they may wonder if something is the matter. However, a delayed rate of physical progress is not necessarily a sign of brain handicap, since the child is learning a lot more about life than just the tasks that show. Warning signs to pay close attention to are eye and ear difficulties, periodic blank stares, unusual body changes, facial contortions, listlessness — symptoms pronounced enough to be observed as continuing, not passing. Repeated or prolonged sounds are common in baby talk, but when they are accompanied by lip tremors, struggle to speak, or "echo words," the matter should be discussed with the family doctor. In the event of doubt, it is better to err on the side of caution and also contact local associations for advice.

Prompt action achieves two things: (1) peace of mind if no serious problem is involved, and (2) the advantage of time to intervene if a developmental disability does exist. It is heartbreaking for parents to learn that their child has been impaired from birth, but for those who had thought that all was well only to discover that it wasn't, the added burdens of guilt, shame and fear have to be brought into the open and talked about so that they aren't misdirected into self-defeating behavior. Unfortunately, some parents, when presented with an accurate diagnosis of brain disorder, have protested it as an affront, or threatened to sue if word got out. Others have felt compelled to search exhaustively for immediate cures, looking more to miracles than to their youngster and themselves. A few may become aloof, take steps to send away what they see as bad news. Only the child remains the same: in need and unaware of any difference.

Underlying such responses is a natural fear about the unknown: the world of institutions and the possibility of having a family member committed to that world. There are of course excellent mental hospitals, as well as circumstances that do mandate confinement. In the main they involve children who have compounding problems beyond the capabilities of parents, residential services or nursing homes. These include profound brain damage, autistic complications that result in continual self-injury, uncontrolled seizures, abrupt reversal of development, serious heart, lung, spinal, kidney and bowel defects. Such extremes are comparatively rare. Even when institutionalization is the sole proper alternative, the decision has to be the parents' — made with the help of informed and caring advice from doctor, social worker and counselor, and by talking things over to assess all options, compassionately reaching acceptance of the inevitable. Where sophisticated treatment is needed to maintain life without hope, parental options must also include the right to no treatment, in the best interests of both family and patient.

Most adult uncertainty about brain handicap, however, arises from the fear that nothing can be done, that the outlook is but a long, arduous road to nowhere. That fear, like many fears, stems from inadequate knowledge and is usually lessened by enlightened counsel. As with early detection, a great deal can be done when symptoms appear later in this second stage. Parents who pull together in the face of challenge gain in emotional strength and love, find new depths of understanding in their efforts to make a better life for their child.

If what they suspect is confirmed and the child does indeed have a developmental disability, there are some preliminaries to deciding upon a course of action. Brain handicap has many different external appearances, depending upon its location, extent and nature, so the first step is a thorough physical examination. If the youngster cannot see or hear adequately, these deficits need correction. The existence of other sensory or motor problems should be looked into and treated, checks made for low thyroid, diabetes, anemia, heart and lung ailments, digestive difficulties, and so forth. Infected tonsils alone have been reported to strain the system enough to interfere with mental capacity. In general, the good health of the child must be secured so that subsequent evaluation is not clouded by some side disorder.

At the same time, the examination should determine *what* developmental disability is involved, along with as precise a definition of its nature as possible. Is it the twitching of chorea that follows rheumatic fever? or the rigidity of dystonia? A simplistic diagnosis of retardation, epilepsy, cerebral palsy or autism demands further specific clarification; for there are several degrees of retardation, numerous patterns of epilepsy, five types of cerebral palsy, varying intensities of autism and multiple causes of each. Moreover, these afflictions may occur separately or together. In case of the latter, parents have more than one handicap to manage. Making the right response depends upon knowing what one is supposed to be responding to, within the framework of full explanation. Professionally qualifying epilepsy as "ideopathic," for instance, meaning "cause unknown," and letting it go at that, just doesn't say enough to those who need helpful elaboration in order to fathom what they face. But an accurate diagnosis, discussed in common terms, goes a long way toward getting home management off to a sound start. By asking questions about what they don't understand, parents can help themselves, the doctor and their child reach that comprehensive starting point.

Once examination and diagnosis are in hand, but before medication is used, the next step is to have a psychological workup. This does not mean that medication should be avoided in situations where it is needed to control seizures or hyperactivity sufficiently to permit the workup. Rather, it means that if the option exists and is advised, an unsedated child has a better chance of demonstrating personal performance levels. Since there are numerous tests — simple movement, word recognition, auditory discrimination, draw-a-person, Bender-Gestalt, and so on — parents should always ask about prices and which tests are most necessary for their child's age. Too, the tester is perhaps of greater significance than the tests; for preliminary measures of IQ

(Verbal, Performance and Full-Scale) in the young must be considered tentative, and the larger observations — emotion and behavior — require the child's cooperation. The younger the child, the more difficult it is to obtain a clear profile. In any event, *no* result should be considered conclusive but only a reflection of a changing picture taken in the spirit of trying to define the total problem and its limitations.

Some psychological tests for the very young are highly interpretive. In one, the child is offered a cookie and observed to take it in either the left or right hand. Then another is offered, which is usually grasped with the free hand. Offering the third poses the dilemma: if the child transfers one cookie to the second hand in order to free the first to accept the extra, this is considered clever; but if the child sets one down, or mouths the third, that is deemed less intelligent. Placing scores on what a youngster decides to do with a cookie, regardless of cultural differences, is a not altogether charming adult amusement. Better are observations on how the child reaches for and holds the cookie, what is done with it, and whether the child responds to or withdraws from the tester.

Every comprehensive evaluation should include a review of the home. Clinical diagnosis remains an abstract if it does not take into account the home environment, character of the parents, and nutritional idiosyncrasies — any one of which can be a contributing factor in brain disorder. The whole-person, whole-family approach is the way to understand all spheres of function — physical, intellectual and emotional — and an accurate, complete case history has to begin with and be based upon individual particulars, free of labels.

Parents generally welcome a nonjudgmental, unbiased review of the home, just as they would welcome anyone who helps make them feel less alone. Those who do allow a careful visit by physician, psychologist or social worker are making a wise decision.

When the resulting case history is written, parents should have the chance to discuss its pertinent findings with the reviewer so that they have some grasp of recommended courses of action and can point out possible oversights. In situations where the review is omitted, parents should request a conference about it, since responsibility for administering medication and programs lies with them, and the more they know, the better chance they have to effect competent management. The parents' right to read the actual case history has been generally established, but it is not, in itself, very productive in most cases. Of greater use is a clear, open and compassionate professional interpretation of what the documents *mean* to parents and their child personally.

Children handicapped in any way are, to varying degrees, penalized in the quality of life experience. They have less opportunity to share, to learn helping behavior, and to use affection. Limited social contact can also reduce their ability to communicate. With brain handicap, the penalty is profound because of its chronic nature. Not only early detection but efforts to remove unnecessary frustrations are important. The process of helping may begin with an evaluation. What happens because of it largely depends upon relaxed parents knowing where they are going and working to go the route together. So the best evaluation is only a preliminary that must be followed up by a flexible program, within reach of family means and abilities and open to modification in the light of trial and error.

For all parents of a developmentally disabled child, the personal impact goes through approximately the same sequence: (1) noticing the problem, (2) trying to find out what it is, (3) despair over confirmation of brain handicap, and (4) reaction to despair. The latter can be minimized by prompt outlining of a good program and open discussion about advances in treatment.

Epilepsy afflicts an estimated thirty million persons worldwide. New drugs are on the market, such as carbamazepine and clonazepam — promising specifics that either complement or replace the dependable regulars, Dilantin and phenobarbital. Potential adverse side effects are being more quickly recognized through improved reporting and research communications. Neurologist David A. Prince of Stanford has been exploring aspects of the role played by neural potassium-sodium balance in seizures. Others have noticed that accompanying anticonvulsants with vitamin C appears to help reduce possible toxicity. There is wider understanding of the relation between brain biochemistry and nutrition, of metabolic errors, and so forth. And the earlier a child is seizure-free, the better the chance of outgrowing epilepsy, avoiding the gratification of dependency during developmental years, or of feeling different, confused, somewhere between sick and well.

In mental retardation, excellent work is being done on training, speech therapy, stimulation, correction of vision and hearing, improvement of personal appearance, dental care, and the fitting of youngsters into regular childhood activities. Through nutritional research on a broad front, it has become apparent that correcting dietary deficits may help to varying degrees. And human rights of the retarded are now protected by law, so parents are no longer backed to the wall.

For cerebral palsy, early corrective therapy can help considerably; and for dyslexia, minimal brain dysfunction and autism, progress is being made with instruction and medication, though assistance to the autistic child could be improved by earlier diagnosis and intervention with sensory stimulation.

Even with all these advances, however, many parents still go through crushing despair. The reactions fall into three general categories: rejection, overprotection — and intelligent acceptance. For those who reject, either by terminating the marriage or by unnecessarily putting their child away, little can be done, apart from encouraging them to try to get together, begin again — for their sake as well as the child's. Not only does every youngster benefit from the security of united parents and the wider stimulation of a happy home, but parents themselves gain in wisdom and stature through the effort to care despite presumed hardships.

Parents who overprotect, on the other hand, should make an effort to realize that their desire to eliminate every conceivable risk, real or imagined, is not so much a positive expression of love as a kind of defense against fear and shame. While indulgence may teach the child to take but not to give, overprotecting tends to create an isolated, immature individual. Some who overprotect can help each other through open talk, expressing the deep feelings we all experience when overwhelmed. It is natural and reasonable for a mother and father to wonder: Was it our fault? Did we do something wrong? It is natural and reasonable for both also to wonder: What will others think? How will this change our lives? Categorically, the *occurrence* of a developmental disability — as opposed to judgmental errors in response — is no one's "fault," no one did anything "wrong," what others may or may not think is immaterial, and how life is changed depends upon the negative or positive courses elected. Which one of us is "perfect"? Life is an exploration, from first to last breath, without any guarantee except that what began will end. So there's a lot to be said for trying to make the most of it, whatever the imponderables, and that can best be done in the absence of fear, working for — not against — each other.

What is more important, the child or the opinion of neighbors? And what kind of an opinion is it, or what kind of friends, that can change because two people are confronted by uncertainty? Aren't we kidding ourselves to respect sunny-day opinions, and aren't we being unfair to friends to limit friendship to pleasant weather or the discussion of it?

Avoidance of overprotection has direct bearing on child development. As an old Hindu proverb puts it, "Nothing grows under the banyan tree." A banyan tree is so sheltering that it takes up most light and moisture, consumes nutrients, becomes a forest unto itself. When parents start becoming human banyan trees, they absorb the experience that every youngster needs for growth. Each of us, regardless of ability, has the right to what is called the dignity of risk — the chance to learn through trial and error, to take our knocks as a way of finding out how to avoid them, to receive credit for successes. Overprotection hurts even the healthiest children, denying them exposure to variety and life in all its possibilities. Confining someone to home out of fear turns home for that individual into a sort of prison; and confinement at an early age can warp the growing mind.

As an extreme example, a small boy became ill with meningitis, which left him deaf and minimally brain damaged. Instead of taking the positive course of trying to help him with his development, the family — perhaps through fear and lack of information — kept him shut up for his "safety," and in so doing unintentionally contributed to his retardation. In less extreme, actually rather common situations — as sometimes may happen with an only child — parental sheltering can result in various unwanted emotional problems.

But overprotection poses some indirect threats, too. The attempt to restrict slows growth and places a greater drain of unending care on parents, which then elevates their hostility so that they are more inclined to regard backwardness as willful. This becomes a vicious circle. The attitude further retards the child and again increases parental hostility, which can't be overtly expressed and so emerges as overambition: the child is expected to progress faster than possible under optimum circumstances, while being loaded down with more restrictions. In a way, it's like asking someone with a ball and chain to run and then putting on another ball and chain because the person doesn't seem to be trying hard enough.

When parents are unable by themselves — for whatever reason — to avoid overprotection, outside counseling helps lead them to an awareness of all the benefits inherent in an attitude of acceptance, patience and tolerance. If counseling is not requested, it can be suggested by either the social worker or family doctor, provided that one or the other is in touch with the home situation and appreciates the fact that professional service isn't going to accomplish much for the child when parents are inadvertently blocking progress.

Once parents have accepted reality, a program of home teaching is of extraordinary use, taking up where infant stimulation left off and giving the mother and father something they can do themselves, thus relieving their own sense of helplessness and replacing it with delightfully creative tasks. Such tasks restore family tranquillity and require no special expertise or unusual means.

As a child reaches the stage of being able to absorb more, a variety of simple instruction helps improve individual visual, auditory and motor skills. In conducting the program, parents should always remember that there are at least two ways of teaching anything. If one way isn't working, it shouldn't be insisted upon or forced. For instance, it's hard for some children with cerebral palsy to walk, impossible for others, and there are those who just don't want to hazard it. Parents who stress that this skill be attained no matter what, placing a high priority on the act, may overlook the child's own priorities, neglect more important things that the child can and wants to do. Also, early concentration on academic learning, to the exclusion of other kinds of learning, tends to inhibit mental development, confusing youngsters with a subject before its relation to life is understood.

In each of the three basic areas — visual, auditory and motor — there is a certain overlap that increases along with complexity. But by and large, visual skills involve activities that use the eyes, auditory skills the ears, and motor skills the body.

To develop visual skills, many items are helpful: pegboards, bingo, blocks, playing cards, dominoes, checkers, tick-tack-toe, Tinkertoys, chalkboard, clay, finger paints, crayons, pictures and words, pictures and numbers. The objective is for mother and father to make something simple and encourage the child to identify salient features by reproducing them, then try to do something independently, using matching colors as well. With pegboard, bingo and tick-tack-toe, the images are two-dimensional and lead eventually to the refinement of games. With items like blocks, dominoes and Tinkertoys, three dimensions through structure are employed. With drawing, the purpose is to develop the abstract of lines in representing concrete images. And with pictures and words and pictures and numbers, the child learns the visual association between image and concept. A bright calendar introduces the connection between numbers and days; a simple cardboard clock with movable hands shows the relation of position, numbers and time — time to eat, time to play, time to sleep.

By beginning simply, with attention to what the child *can* do, and increasing complexity gradually, playfully — letting up when interest wanes — visual stimulation improves total development. Since everyone has individual preferences, there are no hard and fast rules. The items mentioned are only examples. Some families may find home movies and a slide projector resources. Others may want to shop around in toy stores, or send away for a home-school kit. Whatever is used, it should *not* be something that the youngster is given only to play with alone. It should be something that includes the parents in the fine art of visual instruction, while allowing for spontaneous initiation and curiosity on the part of the child.

Increasing auditory skills is achieved through use of different sounds, such as clapping, playing records or the radio, reading aloud, telling fantasy stories, talking, playing with toy phones, chanting nursery rhymes, blowing whistles or whistling, singing, drumming, stamping feet. Most children first delight in any sound made by the mouth — the next step up from nursing, the oral focus still being the center of self through which all things flow — beginning with clicking the tongue, or rocking back and forth to a simple chant.

There are two basic categories of sound: sounds associated with meanings, and sounds associated with pleasure. With the former, "ma" and "da" are in many languages the first verbal identifications of mother and father, but a great amount of other early learning is conceptualized through sound. By holding a child's hand close to something warm and saying "ha," the meaning of "hot" is conveyed, as is the meaning of "cold" by letting a youngster touch an icecube and saying "ko," feeling water called "wa." Words being vibrations from the throat that are varied by the use of the mouth, first knowledge of word sounds is advanced by letting the child touch the throat and mouth as the parent speaks.

In sounds associated with pleasure are all the beginnings of music — the rhythms and tunes that first entertain, then lead to the use of music as a form of communication to express feelings. For the child who does suffer from an auditory impediment, a set of earphones can introduce sounds at a greater volume and can also block out background noises. In many instances of developmental disability, the person doesn't have a hearing deficiency so much as a difficulty in filtering out primary sounds from secondary sounds. Sometimes one ear picks up more than the other; with a stereo system the two can be equalized by balancing left or right, asking the child to indicate when the sound seems to be centered.

As with visuals, the happier the auditory stimulation the better. A home with glad sounds has the same pronounced influence as a home with cheerful colors. And a home with good sounds and visuals helps parents, as well as children, to feel at ease, make the most of the assets they have to work with.

Developing motor skills is problematic when parents are working with a child who has a bone, joint or muscular difficulty. In such instances, a doctor or physical therapist should be consulted for advice on what activities will not overstress an orthopedic limitation. But usually parents can pick from a vast number of things that improve motor stimulation. These range from full body use — swimming, hopping, dancing, skipping, jumping and balancing — to partial or sedentary use, like catching or rolling a ball, playing with tops or jacks, throwing Frisbees, folding, cutting, knitting, blowing up balloons, kneading dough, stacking, sorting, matching, knot-tying, swinging, imitating, playing in a sandbox.

The body benefits from use, not strain. A restricted limb is not going to straighten out by being forced to do what it cannot, but it has a far better chance of improving if surrounding functions are conditioned. Brain development is speeded by increased command of the body and more oxygen circulation through physical exercise. The Roman saying applies: a sound mind in a sound body. For the developing child, this could perhaps be rewritten as the precept: growth through use. Most children are exuberantly active, and parents can give thanks when they are. Brain-handicapped children need extra help to achieve the same end.

In the entire process of home teaching, everyone working with the youngster has to be aware of deficits but not be preoccupied with them to the extent of overlooking the many assets. Each of us is handicapped in one way or another, so winning the battle of life is not a matter of superior fire power or field position but of learning to cope and make the most of what one has to work with. As the American poet Edward Rowland Sill expressed it in his 1887 poem "Opportunity," victory came not to the soldier who threw this sword away because it wasn't good enough but to the oppressed and disarmed warrior who found the broken weapon and turned the tide of battle with it.

Apart from continued sensory stimulation for the child in preschool years, there are points outside the home that must be looked to. A suitable activity center or qualified nursery assists in the development of out-of-home skills and group awareness. An activity center has programs especially for the developmentally disabled, while a nursery is much like prekindergarten. Choosing one or the other depends upon the child's response, not the parents' wish, and the child ought not to be pushed — perhaps just brought to play for an hour once a week, with the mother staying until it's clear that the youngster is ready to enjoy the place without fear of abandonment. That is a security all children need in taking the next step forward.

When communities have no activity centers or nursery schools, a well-run Sunday or Sabbath-day school is an excellent alternative if the program is oriented around group singing and storytelling in a bright, cheerful room. If it has a drama program, so much the better. Imitation, acting out and costuming stimulate role-awareness, the reward being approval from peers and adults. How wonderful it is on special occasions to see the native honesty of youngsters as they participate in dramatization of significant events, for are not we all, regardless of differences, the children of God? Too, in any out-of-home activity, parents are brought together with other parents. This allows for an exchange of information and a sense of ease in getting about publicly with the handicapped. While every parent needs the chance to swap ideas and feel at ease, the need is accentuated for those with a developmentally disabled child.

Added aspects of a good out-of-home schedule include trips to stores, visits to playgrounds, picnics in the park or at the beach, strolls around the neighborhood. The more parents feel comfortable being with their child in social situations, the more the child will feel accepted outside the home, enjoying the advantages of diversified activities. Of course, this emphasizes the importance of attention to and training in matters of appearance and personal dignity. Negative social attitudes toward the developmentally disabled can arise from little more than perceived external differences — clothing, manner, physical awkwardness. But any child who is clean, well-groomed, attractively dressed and secure in the company of loving parents will be appreciated. Early awareness of what makes one socially welcome or unwelcome has a lasting influence upon emerging concepts of self.

The strong arguments *for* out-of-home efforts are much the same as those *against* institutionalization when avoidable. Children kept always at home are denied the wider horizons of life and do not develop well. Any confinement is a form of deprivation. An institution is simply an extreme, unless it has adequate staffing, programs and facilities to permit fully diversified experiences. Put in a place where one is left alone for long periods, denied stimulation and surrounded by monotony from day to day, how can *any* individual be expected to flourish, physically or mentally?

When the Developmental Disabilities Act was passed and the direction of treatment swung toward in-community living, the public began to see the host of human beings, like released prisoners of war, withered and bewildered, who had been denied personal rights because they were powerless to advocate for or defend themselves. In case after case, the impact of neglect was apparent, as was the potential of reversing it to various degrees through increased stimulation and broader experience.

To cite one example, a mentally retarded young man — in his early thirties but looking around sixty because he had no teeth and could not eat properly — was released after having been needlessly shut away since boyhood. The record stated that he was "low-grade moron," violent, unable to speak, with an attention span of five seconds. The head nurse also advised, off the record, that his fearful behavior made her believe that he was possessed by demons and had best be kept regularly sedated. Outside the hospital, he was found to be loving, with a devotion to those who showed him kindness and affection. Using that devotion, caseworkers were able to teach him to speak, write his name, groom himself and use a set of false teeth. The first clue that he could talk came when he was taken to the beach for a picnic. He had never seen the ocean, but at the sight of it he spread his arms in a moving expression of gratitude and said, "O-shun." His memory of individuals who accepted him was long, and his attention span at mechanical tasks, plus an uncanny knack with machinery, enabled him to be trained *and* employed as a service station attendant. Whatever had happened in the understaffed institution, he had conformed there to the behavior that others expected of him.

Realistically, the outlook in all but extreme situations is hopeful and clearly aided by alert parents, professionals and others working with the handicapped person in nonrestrictive environments. To complement the many positive things possible in and around the home, parents can be relieved of financial anxieties by early anticipation of long-range needs.

Taking out family medical insurance is a must, even without chronic health problems. Yet according to Senator Edward Kennedy, forty million Americans have no health insurance, and for many others coverage may be inadequate. Information about Supplemental Security Income (SSI) and Medicare programs defines what assistance is available and what isn't. Some medical clinics offer plans whereby parents pay a small monthly amount that then takes care of every professional fee. There is even help for travel through Greyhound's exemplary Helping Hand Service, which parents should ask about if they lack other forms of transportation.

But in addition to coverage for expected and unexpected costs, another useful type of insurance is an endowment policy for each child, as well as life insurance policies for the parents. Life insurance with a designated guardian or trustee protects the child in the event that one or both parents die. Endowment — applicable where families are ineligible for SSI — is taken out for the child to provide a monthly sum on reaching adulthood that will help with training and education. If it is not needed at that time, payments can be put into a second endowment. Parents who can afford to part with fifteen percent of their income will save by paying into a tax-deductible IRA (Individual Retirement Account), naming children as beneficiaries, or purchasing stocks and bonds for each child, under the Uniform Gift to Minors Act. Since the various considerations require careful study, much can be clarified in terms of individual family needs and means by talking things over with a helpful insurance agent, banker, certified public accountant, or investment counselor.

In other words, comprehensive financing goes right along with every other aspect of a comprehensive approach to developmental disabilities. Nothing can be overlooked.

▣ The Parents

CONTINUING CARE OF A BRAIN-HANDICAPPED CHILD in the family rests largely with the parents, who are often expected to remain steadfast though unaided, when in fact they need help and understanding almost as much as their youngster does. "Help" does not necessarily mean physical assistance or a prescription to calm the nerves, unless medically advised. It means concerned, informed, caring, *early* counsel on what to do and how to do it. In the absence of this, two people are left to sink or swim and at the same time try to devise the right program for a complex disability with which they've had no prior experience. It is comfortable to say, "They'll get used to it." Far from getting used to anything, they may become more prone to believe in the myth of the "problemless life."

Like the myth of normality, the belief that certain people have no problems came to be through fear of differences and social inducements to evade rather than express real feelings that might make the differences more apparent. Perhaps this traces to the superstition that exposure of any weakness, physical or spiritual, brought bad luck by calling attention to it. Whatever the source, the convention perists in various circles that only niceties should be discussed and that there is something improper, or at least unpleasant, about emotional reality. Suppression of meaningful talk furthers the illusion that deep personal predicaments are rare, that anyone so burdened not only is an exception but quite possibly is being punished for secret wrongdoing. The truth is that depression has now become the most common emotional complaint in affluent societies and suicide a leading cause of death.

Like everyone else, parents of a developmentally disabled youngster — and I speak as such a parent — often feel backed to the wall, and talking about problems can appear unusually difficult. On the one hand, friends and neighbors may seem blessed with comparatively few common complaints; on the other, how can one take the lighthearted attitude that troubles ignored will disappear? The exposed and supposed weakness *is* the child. It's impossible simply to turn away, as if quitting an unsatisfactory job, or successfully engage in polite evasions. Without kind assistance, afflicted parents are more apt than others to slip into one of the six patterns of counterproductive behavior: overprotection, undue anxiety, social inhibition, blame-fixing, escapism and scapegoating. However, by being aware of these patterns, as well as their early signs and underlying causes, most of us can usually help ourselves through open discussion of the very emotions that seem too painful to admit. For each of us — regardless of circumstance — gains by discussing real feelings, by trying to look at things for what they are, not what one might wish them to be, and to understand that what seems to be *not* understandable begins with the never finished task of understanding self. No matter how the word is turned, no matter how the thought is phrased, the challenge of life evolves from this fundamental reality.

As mentioned previously, overprotection encompasses a range of excesses, from too much clothing in cold weather to bed treatment for minor complaints. Such behavior is bad for the child's development. It is no less unhealthy for parents, involving them in ceaseless remedies of a "do-not" nature. Without realizing it, they slowly build up a dependence upon the handicap in a way that can negatively structure their lives. The unexpressed *real* feeling here is not worry but a wish to be free of the child — a wish so strong that it seems unbearable to face, must constantly be denied by protective actions that protect only the wish from being grappled with by the parents. After all, how can one easily say, "May God forgive me, I sometimes feel that I want to be free of my child"? But *saying* so doesn't *make* it so, and surely the wish won't go away if allowed to remain untouched, growing every day that it is not confronted.

Undue anxiety involves a high level of tension that emanates from repressed anger, usually about the extra work involved in caring for a handicapped child, but sometimes about the slowness or uncertainties of progress, the common ups and downs that seem so trying. Instead of accepting the fact that anger exists and looking to constructive uses of it, parents may fear as wrong *any* show of simple hostility, including annoyance, toward their disabled youngster. As feelings denied then accumulate under the cloak of self-control, they tend to escape through the safety valve of nervous symptoms: headaches, shallow sleep, intestinal upsets, frequent calls to the doctor about minor things, the disorganized activities of getting "wound up like a top." Since there appears to be too much to do, basics are more readily overlooked. The home may be piled with unwashed clothes and bedding, in which the youngster wanders aimlessly while the parents are trapped in peripheral duties, or are so worn out that even little tasks are exhausting. I've observed that some children raised in such surroundings either become subdued or develop a set of nervous responses of their own. At the other extreme, the house may always be so immaculate that no one can relax and play in it. Each time that hidden emotions are not expressed makes it harder to bring them to the surface. Tension also hammers in the wedge to split the marriage; for if two people cause each other enough unpleasantness, they will sooner or later begin to blame the relation as the *source* of it. But when they try from the first to be honest about natural anger and frustration, talking things over without fear, they have a much better chance of avoiding many adverse consequences.

Social inhibitions are marked by the parents' reluctance to accept or extend invitations. Here, the unfaced feeling is shame of brain handicap. Overtly, they may say that they can't afford to entertain and so don't wish to be obligated, or they develop another rationale, such as a specialized diet, to justify the stance. In some instances only one parent goes out at a time, the other staying behind. Whatever the course, the result is limited social contact, which denies parents necessary variety, confirms their unacceptability and deepens their sense of shame. When the insular pattern becomes habit, it is very difficult for a social worker to make a house call and manage to get beyond the front door. Parents like this can drift into separation, but mostly they acquire a Hansel and Gretel dependence upon each other, often seeking total solitude. To reverse this lonely trend, they need to recognize that there is nothing wrong with feeling ashamed and saying so freely as a preface to finding ways of enjoying company.

Blame-fixing is a domestic entertainment conducted at the top of the lungs and inspired by hidden guilt. It creates its own nuances and satisfactions fostered by the notion that life without conflict is dull. The drama begins following a stressful moment with the child, or some associated demand. An insecure man has difficulty accepting responsibility for "imperfect" offspring. Since the mother carried the baby and it came from her, obviously she's at fault. Either she did something stupid, or her family had an overload of skeletons rattling around in the closet. In defense, the woman acquires the art of keeping book on every transgression, large or small, that she can pin on her husband. The ensuing verbal battle vents frustrations but rarely eases the source of guilt and always emotionally wounds the child. Eliminating such situations requires a period of mutual confession so both parents can see that *neither* is at fault, that *neither* did anything wrong, and that there is more rewarding stimulation in meeting challenges together than in periodically clashing about them.

Escapism also traces to unfaced guilt. We *all* need occasional relief from daily demands to help us approach them with a refreshed spirit, but symptomatic escapism is a compulsion. One route is alcohol. Drinking becomes progressively heavier and more self-destructive. Oblivion is the aim, elevation of guilt the aftermath — and thus the next round. If the nutrition and care of the parent are neglected, so are those of the child. Another route is evasion: taking on an exhaustive schedule of community responsibilities to help forget about those at home. In moderation, both alcohol and community service may be desirable. But establishing what individual levels are best for a given family again requires parents to be aware of guilt and come to grips with it before escapism grows to unmanageable proportions to the further detriment of their developmentally disabled child. Indeed, even to call for outside counsel when necessary, parents first have to have the humility to identify their sometimes embarrassingly true feelings.

Scapegoating is another avenue for relieving guilt. In this, practically everyone else is to blame, or at least seems so — doctors, teachers, social workers, neighbors. Since no one can do anything right, no one wishes to try, and the withdrawal of assistance is viewed as confirmation of hostile intent. The original story of the scapegoat comes from the Bible, when Abraham decided that he would have to make atonement by sacrificing his only son to God. Then in the nick of time, a goat appeared trapped in the bushes and was offered instead.

Latter-day scapegoating may be a long way from ritual sacrifice, but it still derives from the ancient belief that when life seems unbearable, the hardship is punishment for sin, and guilt is relieved by placing blame on another life. Meanwhile, the brain-handicapped child experiences less care, along with negative training in attitudes toward people. What parents need to do when the whole world starts to look so wrong is to look to themselves and try to express the seemingly inexpressible.

We are all acquainted with feelings of grief, guilt, fear, shame, anger and hatred, as well as their positive opposites. And there is no one on earth who does not require, at one time or another, some help in putting such feelings into perspective when they become intense enough to exclude a sense of balance. Regardless of one's religious commitment, an informed minister, priest or rabbi can often point in the right direction, aware of appropriate counseling services while extending spiritual comfort, forgiveness and blessings.

So much favors the course of parents talking openly with each other from the start, speaking of what is most painful, touching the wound in order to heal it. They are like two eyes in one head. Each has to see clearly for perspective. To face the truth and know it severs the bondage of evasion, opens the way to discovery of other truths. To turn away only feeds and perpetuates anguish. Parents who speak to each other of realities lighten their burdens and deepen the marriage. For parenthood is a developmental process — an active joy of giving — which doesn't cease when the children grow up. But where avenues of communication have been closed, mother and father need help, and many are the ways by which they can be guided.

If early intervention is good for the child, it is good for the parents, too. Any physician serving a family with a developmental disability should have a list of community agencies and refer the case at once to a social worker for evaluation to prevent stress in the home before it occurs or to reduce it as soon as possible. In places where there are no social workers, a qualified public health nurse can assist; and where there are no public health nurses, a local religious institution may be useful.

The deepest isolation parents face occurs right after the diagnosis, whether at birth or later on. To be advised that one's child has a brain handicap may sound like the pronouncement of some sort of sentence, even when cushioned by understanding explanation. One hears the words, but they suddenly seem far-off and unreal, as one is caught up in a swirl of questions: Why did this happen? How serious is it? Is there any hope? What are we to do? In those first bewildering moments, which may endure for days, direct emotional support and counsel on available services is of extraordinary, urgent importance to encourage a realistic view of the child on individual merits and to avoid any possibility that parents might accept incorrect advice from informal sources.

Neighbors able to rally around a family that has been left homeless or sustained a tragic physical accident can extend the same compassion to those who have just been confronted by a developmental disability if they simply offer the comfort of friendship rather than try to make suggestions about what they don't know. For each child has special needs that are best evaluated by someone experienced in the field. One exemplary program, described in the November 1976 issue of *Modern Medicine of Canada*, is called Pilot Parents (see *Agencies*, listed at the end of this book). Started in Toronto, the program now has branches in other parts of Canada and uses trained parents, who themselves have handicapped youngsters, to aid parents newly coping with the disability. One hopes that the organization will in time reach other nations.

In reviewing the family situation, parents require a program of things they can do, in and out of home, to help their child, using available resources, as they make the transition from anxiety to confident management. We don't expect people to drive a car without some training at it. Far less should we expect someone to know all about managing brain handicap without guidance. As with early care, every minute of early guidance is worth an hour of later redirection. To embark upon an understandable course is tonic for the parents, and the beginnings of their open communication lie in concerted action. The social worker can spot housing and financial problems, suggest the means of solving them. But since aloneness is a factor at the onset of brain handicap, it is equally useful to review the availability of friends in the community, as well as referring to sources of new contact, particularly with local developmental disability associations; for one aftermath of aloneness is a sense of estrangement — a feeling of not really being part of anything — and the sooner it is interdicted by exposure to areas of shared concern, the less chance it has of becoming chronic.

Most parents have an opportunity to enjoy occasional moments by themselves outside the home. This is good for them and their child. Those caring for a disabled youngster, however, may feel that they can't take a break, even if they do know of a competent baby-sitter. Yet the very quality of their care depends upon periodic time out from parenting.

One solution is to ask grandparents to hold the fort for awhile. Another is to send the child to visit a friend or relative overnight, perhaps locate a respite care service for weekends. When the mother is unable to work, or is housebound tending to young children, some schedule has to be arranged for the father to spell her regularly to keep her from getting cabin fever. In families where extra income earned by a working mother is imperative to making ends meet, a free day-care center has to be found, or there must be work that she can take in. Where neither option is available, the social worker must secure direct financial aid without delay.

Vacations are another consideration. The occurrence of a developmental disability inclines many parents to feel that the style of their holidays has to be revised — that they can only go places and do things that are not awkward and keep the child within reach of medical assistance. Actually, one of the healthiest and least expensive forms is a camping trip — by car, boat, cabin, backpack — where there are no services, let alone medical. Everyone needs a change of scene. It is mandatory when daily routine is fixed around brain handicap.

The words "housing and financial difficulties" aren't merely polite terms for squalor and poverty. Poor parents don't have to be destitute, and low-income housing doesn't have to be squalid. But where the landlord is overcharging for and not maintaining the property, the social worker can bring the full weight of government to bear and simultaneously help the family look to alternate housing. In some instances, parents may have a debt burden that should be lightened by refinancing. In others, lack of a workable budget leads to overspending on the wrong things at the wrong time — a propensity that calls for counsel on financial planning. People trying to manage under hardship are often those in need of help in changing patterns that only make their living situation worse, and the skilled social worker can do much by spotting these patterns early on.

The poor have access to public assistance, and the wealthy to tax shelters, but those in the middle — our vast majority — have no fallback from the struggle of trying to pay for themselves while being taxed to pay for others. A family earning $12,000 a year pays out at least twenty-five percent in income, property and sales taxes, the equivalent of three months' work, on top of the labor of delivering special care for which there is no extra deduction. Since they are ineligible for assistance, the balance is swiftly consumed, and inflation eats away at what they can do. Here, a housing problem takes on a different character — that of suburban sameness with a crushing property tax base, to which the family feels tied because of the father's job. The escape for them is to forget status and move to quarters with a lower tax and maintenance cost, and reduced transportation expenses. Yet again, those under the crunch may lack the time or confidence to see and act upon options without assistance.

Specialized counseling, as distinguished from professional advice, is called for in the face of existing marital strife, or when parents begin blocking real communication. Mother and father can become overwhelmed without being aware of it, simply by having extended themselves daily beyond the point of endurance: care for another may seem so much a way of life that parents have to be reminded to care for each other. Specialized counseling need not involve formal sessions on the couch, or group psychotherapy, or other means of getting those who have evaded reality to start looking at it. Rather, it often involves a conference with someone trained to identify unrealistic responses to a developmental disability and capable of suggesting corrective approaches. Every social worker should have a list of qualified counselors and know when to refer (and when not to) so that parents don't wind up with someone who, with the best of intentions, does more harm than good trying to relate current problems to ancient woes, taking up time and money only to add to the burden inadvertently. The keystone of health delivery to the child *is* mother and father. If one or both go down, where then shall the youngster live, and who assumes the responsibilities? Yet obvious as this seems, there is still a tendency to regard parents as incidental to the system, when instead they should be aided as focal to it.

In the absence of a home program, activities tend to drift off on unsuccessful tangents. Some families may even associate every setback — from toothaches to spilled milk — with the developmental disability. It is all too easy to interpret the wear and tear that can happen to anyone as being caused by a persistent worry. But a regular schedule of productive activities — walks, talks, games — helps avoid the inclination to become habituated to watching, waiting and brooding. Often, the introduction of a household pet offers stimulation to the child and happy distraction to the parents (though it must be kept in mind that a good pet takes time, costs money, and is an added responsibility deserving of love, not something to be discarded when inconvenient).

An adequate response to a developmental disability thus includes not just some but *all* aspects of parental activity: medical care, the environment, home, finances, nutrition, work, vacations, counseling, programs, associations.

The morale of the family is where it's at, for there isn't anyone who can do the job with as much significance to the child as an informed, reassured mother and father, working together in the spirit of patience and understanding. While I've suggested a Bill of Rights for children earlier, I've often felt that it's just as important to recognize some Beatitudes for parents:

Blessed are they who try,
> for they shall be fulfilled.

Blessed are they who love,
> for they shall find comfort.

Blessed are they who cherish truth,
> for they shall gain wisdom.

Blessed are they who stand in faith,
> for they shall be uplifted.

Blessed are they who seek,
> for they shall find new ways.

Blessed are they who forgive,
> for they shall know understanding.

Blessed are they who trust,
> for they shall be honored.

Blessed are they who share,
> for they shall discover abundance.

Blessed are the kind,
> for they shall triumph over ignorance.

Money may be the gateway to "success." It isn't even the keyhole to the abode of morale. The most expensive treatment on earth will falter without the medicine of morale, while the simplest flourishes under its healing balm. Such a state is not so much the fortress of advantage as the place of gladness, the spirit of fairness, the will to press on, and it begins with the shared direction of parents, who look to what they can do for themselves and others, not to what has been done unto them — look to answers, not faulting the world because something didn't work out.

The way family morale aids treatment of brain handicap is no great mystery. It is identical to the way that optimum growth is provided for every child by improving the quality of sensory awareness. When a child is picked up with appreciation, that child experiences being appreciated. When comforted through tears, the child knows comfort. When disciplined fairly, a child understands fairness. When play is fun, activities are happy. When bedtime is pleasant, sleep is welcome. When there is laughter in the house, there is joy at heart. But above all, mother and father become the source of real security. To a youngster, it doesn't make any difference whether parents are rich or poor, dull or smart, handsome or homely, "important" or "unimportant." If they are kind to each other, home is stable, and within that stability they are the most beautiful, important people on earth.

If good morale in the family directly aids treatment, depression and fear impede it. No one grows up well without a lot of TLC; and someone who becomes a destructive adult just didn't suddenly get there alone, the myth of spontaneous corruption notwithstanding. When a child is irritably handled, that child experiences rejection. When neglected, the child knows neglect. When punishment is harsh and unfair, a child learns to deceive. When play is a bother, activities become hostile. When bedtime is captiously enforced, night is a threat. When there is anger in the house, there is fear at heart. And if things are not right between mother and father, the child faces constant uncertainty, responding with behavior designed to perpetuate dependence and keep parents together. To them, the youngster then becomes a daily reminder that they are "trapped" by a financial liability, that but for the trap they could be "free" to do other things gratifying to them.

Within the family, parents are not just the providers of love, they are the *origin* of it. Love does not mean the absence of disagreements or saccharine denials of them. It means the honest attempt to resolve disagreements. Love is never an accomplished fact. It is a direction worked at. Love is not freedom from problems or negative feelings. It is a formidable construct of positive values, of tender intimacy and respect, built up by two people, step by step, care by care.

Agreeing on the precepts of child-raising is perhaps a whole lot more important as a preface to marriage than agreeing on money, politics and other matters. For child-raising is a touchstone of love. When love reigns in the home, hard tasks become easier and no day is too long. There is appreciation for things done well, enjoyment of each other and mutual assistance in the face of challenge. Any guests then enter an atmosphere of acceptance whose direct measure is a feeling of being at ease.

The child who grows up in this atmosphere has the best chance of thriving from day to day, physically and mentally. Emotional security is enhanced, as is the influence on IQ during the crucial labors of developing a whole and meaningful sense of self. Like a plant watered, tended and appreciated, a child blossoms under the gentle sun and rain of loving care.

The example of autism may be pertinent. This brain handicap is sometimes blamed on parental aloofness. Blame only injures parents seeking help and can negate their efforts for the child. Like calling a symptom of anxiety "psychosomatic" and letting it go at that, the bare diagnosis may have a clinical basis but lacks applied value unless it is accompanied by constructive alternatives. With autism, auditory stimuli are distorted to the extent that the brain's processing centers either confuse the decoding of sounds or are unable to screen and select, quite possibly because the centers themselves are activated and creating stimuli of their own without relation to reality. The resulting clinical features are variable: withdrawal, resistance to change, repetitive sounds and acts, sudden distress for no apparent reason, impaired intellectual development, problems with eye use, and either listlessness or overactivity. Thus the child may rock back and forth, oblivious to the world, as if hearkening to some internal rhythm, but will quickly put things back the way they were if set surroundings, such as an arrangement of blocks, are changed. And in talking, syllables may be coupled on a matching basis, like a sort of foreign language that only experienced parents can interpret. Some of these children show distress when talked to directly but enjoy listening to a story told to someone else. Since no effective treatment for autism has yet been discovered, the paramount need is to treat the parents and the person, not the symptoms. Parents of autistic children, for the child's sake, need all the reassurance possible. They also need a program of what they can do at home, as well as a set of community activities to improve their own spirit and open the door to the exercise of workable individual options.

Cerebral palsy is, by contrast, a form of brain handicap in which the importance of home happens to be better appreciated because physical care depends so strongly and obviously *on* the home. Here, damage from birth results in reduced control of head, arms and legs. Clinically, there are several different types, though the technicalities don't mean much to parents, who mainly want to know what they can do to improve life for their child. There is fortunately a great deal, including infant sensory stimulation, that can prevent deterioration and lead to a creative existence, though it requires parents to revise their own priorities and place the growth of intellect above pushing for physical performance. For overall treatment, parents should study the excellent handbook by Nancie R. Finnie, *Handling the Young Cerebral Palsied Child at Home*, which details exercises, basics and precautions.

Every aspect of best management of every developmental disability begins with parents, from whom each of us learns the joy of living through the early seeds of direction. Any medical, social or educational program that overlooks the role of parents must operate at a disadvantage. A child's first awareness of self, and reduction of aloneness, comes through the loving physical contact of parents, natural or foster. And parents greatly improve that contact if helped from the first to eliminate fears as they learn to play an active, intelligent part in total treatment.

Being parents is a curious contradiction of social values: you *pay* for the privilege of doing the work, but don't in the end get to *keep* what you worked so hard at if you did it successfully. Yet in the enigma also lies the entire significance of human endeavor. Who would have it otherwise?

◼ Brothers and Sisters

For Teachers

IN ROOM ONE OF THE ELEMENTARY SCHOOL, ANDY plays well, is a joy to teach, yet complains of stomachaches that require rest. In room two, Jane is neat and courteous, a "little mother" in her relations, but is often tired. In room three, Doug is a classic disruption, with a seemingly inexhaustible knack for getting attention. And in room four, Susan is considered outstanding, though her work is curiously uneven.

While these four children are quite different, coming from various backgrounds, each has one thing in common: a brain-handicapped brother or sister at home. Andy gets stomachaches because he has overheard his parents worrying about "autism"; Jane tires because work for her begins *after* school, when she takes care of her retarded brother; Doug craves attention, since most of it goes to his cerebral palsied sister; and Susan ponders the meaning of what she cannot ask about in view of her family's refusal to discuss the word "epilepsy."

There are over twelve million Andys, Janes, Dougs and Susans in the United States — the forgotten children expected not only to grow up by themselves but to remain untouched by the label placed on one of their own. Each knows that something is not right, wonders how much it is a part of self, senses strangeness among friends. If these worries are ignored, they only grow deeper. But if they are handled intelligently, the earlier such children learn the facts, the easier their own lives — and those of their parents — will be.

Terms like "developmental disabilities" are mouthful enough for adults, never mind youngsters. However, there is no reason why some aspects of how the human brain works cannot be usefully explained to little ones, helping them understand that the signs of brain handicap are not something to be afraid of, that everything known or done is governed by the central nervous system. Schools are supposed to be in the business of teaching minds, so it might be a good idea to start with what is being taught.

Of course, *any* serious handicap, of whatever nature, is a continuing concern to members of the immediate family. But brain disorders are also obscured by prejudice, and understanding from an early age is the way to bring about change, to relieve those afflicted. For the unendurable does not come from the disability, it is *created* by ignorance.

Nowadays, special education classes are available to the developmentally disabled. These single such children out in the eyes of their peers as "them" and contribute to the anxieties of their brothers and sisters, whose well-being is incumbent upon the teachers of regular classes. There are few guidelines to help, though the first step is to define the situation: what is really the matter and why? Stomachaches, fatigue, attention-getting actions and uneven work can be symptoms of other stress at home — divorce, a medical crisis, an impending move, financial difficulties. Most of these surface with relative ease when the teacher takes the time to ask privately "How are your mother and father?" or "Did you enjoy supper last night?" A friendly question usually reveals much, when conversation is followed up in the same spirit. Any family problem has to be understood if the teacher is to interact appropriately with the child and interpret classroom behavior. Sometimes parents volunteer information with a note or phone call. It's when evasions occur and the difficulty persists that the teacher should look to the possible existence of a brain-injured sibling.

Even with a supportive parental attitude, the child may feel hesitant to talk about it, beyond admitting that perhaps one brother or sister is a little different. A destructive attitude, on the other hand, can make for evasions so deep that the process of discovery has to be circuitous: Do both parents work? What do they like to do? How many brothers and sisters? What do they like to do? This line of questioning determines the numbers and names of other children. The one that *isn't* talked about requires the teacher's special concern. There's no urgency to get finite answers, because the objective is the child's trust in an area that the child has been taught to fear — taught sufficiently, in some cases, to become a potential ringleader in teasing someone with an *un*-concealed handicap. These children have to unfold in their own way and will do so slowly, as if learning to walk, taking one uncertain step after another, reaching for open arms, gaining confidence that they will not be left to fall.

Next comes knowledge of the mother's outlook. Chances are she feels alone because the father is preoccupied with *his* work, assuming that the kids are *her* work. To elicit his increased participation, she may make demands of him that strain the marriage, further adding to worries among her other children. Adversity can often cement relations if both parents meet it with open minds, but sometimes divorce may already have prefaced the teacher's exposure to an upset child in the class. In all instances, the teacher can compensate to an important degree through conferences with the mother, by extending acceptance, trying to include the father, pointing to the many positive things being done. A calm mother at home is a decided asset to any classroom.

The third point is to be aware, as I have discussed in the previous chapter, of hidden parental guilts and angers that can be associated with caring for a brain-handicapped youngster. There is no reason to tread on either, to play psychiatrist, or even to suggest family counseling. Some parents labor under such an emotional burden that they refuse to accept the word "retarded" and prefer to use substitute terms that can be reduced to capital letters. Others may be overly involved in organizations designed to do something about everything but home. A few displace anger by treating the disabled child as a pet while placing unreasonable discipline on brothers and sisters. And others, like the parents of Jane in room two, may put the backwork on the kids. In the April 1972 issue of *Psychology Today*, a survey revealed that children adversely affected were themselves afraid of being impaired in some way and experienced guilt about their negative feelings toward parents and handicapped sibling, while those who benefited had learned tolerance and compassion. The teacher cannot change what exists at home but, by being aware of the situation, can show the pupil another way, show the child that life is a gift on loan, that problems are opportunities for insight if talked about and understood.

Fourth, a great deal of attention is usually given, in various forms, to the handicapped youngster. The result often is that parents subtly neglect each other and the rest of the family, forgetting that everyone needs to be loved, to be rewarded or punished fairly, to be listened to. We all worry about the one unwell in our family. But in the case of a developmental disability, the worry can sometimes be all day, every day, with no end in sight. By not being personally involved with the anxiety, the teacher is better able to give attention to the child in need of it, rather than clamping down on attention-getting; for a few minutes of direct affection saves hours of indirect correction. Affection does not undermine authority. It is the basis of it. Lack of caring sets the stage for disruption.

Fifth, it is the democratic heritage to minimize, at least nominally, the influence of money and social status. We Americans believe in one nation, indivisible, with liberty and allied virtues for all. But the way things work out, the family with money and a spacious home has an advantage in coping with brain handicap over those limited by space, money and time. The wealthy can afford the best home care or private residential service; the poor cannot but are aided by government programs that give them priority. Those neither rich nor poor are hardest hit. They do not qualify for assistance, they do not have the means to hire maids or pay for private services, they live in areas where conformity and achievement are at a premium, and they have been brought up with a drive to be self-dependent. Since it is not possible to conform, achieve or be independent with a brain-handicapped child, this is where the pressures are most profound and, accordingly, where the impact on the well child most grave. If a social worker can be of real help here, so can the teacher — not with the family but with the child in class, guiding the youngster to personal concepts of achievement, independence, purpose and self-confidence.

And sixth, despite the best efforts of Women's Liberation, there still remain sharp differences between parental expectations of boys and girls, their roles and duties. In many families, the brothers of a handicapped child are relieved from what is considered "woman's" work, while the sisters are expected to take over for Mother. Jane in room two may be exhausted from doing her mother's work, but Andy in room one happens to have a sister who is equally hard-pressed and needs to know not just that he is related but how he belongs in terms of what he can do — both for his autistic brother *and* for his overworked sister. The teacher can assist him and other students by explaining that it is not unmanly for boys to baby-sit or enjoy cooking, cleaning and making beds, that gender has little to do with rigidly prescribed roles but grows from being strong enough to pitch in for those you love.

Newton once postulated that for every action there is an equal and opposite reaction. His formula — $F=MA$ — came about, according to legend, from watching apples fall. The teacher is in a position to watch the occurrence of something far more significant than falling apples and postulating a new theory of human endeavor. If learned by children from the start, it is a lesson that stays with them throughout their following years of development: that for every situation there is an equal and opposite compensation. Adversity can be turned to advantage, strengthening character, converting problems into learning experiences. This is especially so with brain handicap, when the role of the mind is talked about, and what happens when something works differently in it is explained. The great opportunity is to teach tolerance by discussing attitudes, asking each child to think about what is meant by normal, and by giving and comparing examples of the term.

The story of Adam and Eve may not be so much an attempt to explain the beginning of mankind as a parable of growing up: we are born to innocence, and all is provided for; then we take the first confusing bite of knowledge, and innocence is gone. We become uncertainly aware, and the garden of childhood is no more. Once-omnipotent adults are seen as individuals, humanly limited, grappling with imponderables and their own wounds of childhood, and it becomes time — as time itself hastens — to leave, to go out and, hopefully, to know more.

The brothers and sisters of brain-handicapped children, the other special ones, are perhaps thrust out of the Garden of Eden sooner than most. Finding and taking their hands is a way of teaching life, of trying to make the transition better for all.

For Parents

Signs of sibling stress are often harder to detect at home than at school because they are so much a part of the daily scene that they don't seem to stand out. But when parents do become aware of some problem, or are advised of it, scolding is not the answer. Sitting down and working things out is.

For instance, the kindness and understanding of the well-known actor Spencer Tracy, and his wife, Louise, was not only good for their first son, John, born deaf, it formed the basis of loving appreciation of him by his sister Susie. Moreover, working with John in a spirit that included Susie, Mrs. Tracy went on to establish a school for other children with hearing disabilities. Much good was thus accomplished on a very broad front, and it began with the parental attitude of trying to respond as helpfully as possible.

Perhaps the main consideration for families with a developmentally disabled youngster is to make an effort, to whatever extent individually feasible, to respond *both* comprehensively and inclusively, avoiding preoccupation with the handicap in a manner that renders everything and everyone else secondary. For certainly, such preoccupations are not healthy for the handicapped youngster, who may learn to see all gratification as a function of dependency, refusing encouragement toward independence, and it is decidedly unhealthy for the brothers and sisters. Their neglect may cause long-term personality problems as they endeavor in an erratic way to relieve frustrations and somehow gain the care necessary for *their* best development. Such behavior adds to the strain on parents. It also denies the handicapped child stimulation from happy brothers and sisters.

The claim that families in need tend to manifest personality flaws is a gross oversimplification. Families in need are families in need, period. How those needs emerge cannot be so superficially generalized, for individual particulars vary from situation to situation, depending upon character and circumstance. But when chronic anxiety or other stress-related factors do begin to take an evident toll, problems can be ameliorated by the sympathetic counseling of a specialist well trained in this field. Such a counselor avoids sweeping pronouncements and instead observes specific family patterns before suggesting corrective changes in the home program.

By being aware of sibling concerns, which sometimes may be indirectly expressed, parents themselves can often initiate helpful responses. For them to do so, it is imperative that they understand both the usual and unusual aspects in the task of growing up today. The usual ones are those that have always confronted any child developing in any age. While it is popular to regard childhood, from a forgetful adult standpoint, as a blissful, happy, carefree period, in reality children experience many grave feelings associated with fear, identity, guilt, anger, doubt and nascent sexuality. Throughout the developmental years, every youngster experiences an almost ceaseless internal struggle with troublesome thoughts arising from increased self-awareness. Thus "boogeymen" project fear — usually fear of losing parents through separation, death, departure. In objective terms, no threat may exist, but the threat is nonetheless "real" because it *is* felt, which makes that feeling part of emotional reality. Similarly, the growth of identity involves a process of discovery, learning through trial and error about behavior that results in acceptance or rejection from others within changing, undefined concepts of "popularity." What may seem to parents only a minor slight can to the youngsters be a tear-provoking incident because it touches so painfully on the vital but unclear sense of self. Guilt, generally regarded as an adult emotion, is another strong childhood feeling, often based on fantasy or distorted reality. Actions begin to be known not just as pleasant or unpleasant but as right and wrong, with gradations in between that create difficult choices accompanied by a deep sense of guilt, the child troubled about possible sanctions from sources unknown. Expressions of anger, too, take many forms among kids, ranging from subtle attempts at "getting even" to full-scale outbursts. To the extent that these emotions are repressed, and the sources of frustration remain unrelieved, they further add to internal difficulty and confusion. As for childhood doubt or shame, such feelings usually arise from some exposed inadequacy, actual or presumed. The common taunt, "My dad can lick yours," isn't simply intended to arrange a contest between fathers but relates to awareness of shame and youthful attempts to use or cope with it, putting someone down while trying to avoid being put down. Finally, sex is, of course, very much a part of childhood — a potent force in countless ways, from infancy through adolescence (and beyond). The emotional quotient here rises when the need to know is circumscribed by social concepts of what is right and proper to know.

These psychological components of childhood are universal and have always existed. But today there are many unusual compounding factors that have to be clearly grasped if parents are to be wisely supportive. The fear of losing parents is no longer a matter of boogeymen and goblins. It is a living aspect of the way in which the extended peer group has replaced the extended family — the stable circle of cousins, grandparents, uncles and aunts living nearby and interacting on a continuing basis. An extended family (of which the television show "The Waltons" is reminiscent) offered the buffer of familiarity and security against childhood fears, with associations not all of the same age but ranging from young to old. This made it easier for the parents of a developmentally disabled child, since the family *was* the community and the task of care was *not* conducted in social isolation. But as modes of transportation became mechanized, people could live at a greater distance from work, move about the country to job or place of choice, and the extended family slowly vanished.

Into this vacuum moved the extended peer group — the loose association of those the same age, as brought along by schools. To be part of the community thus now means being part of an age level, with a lessening of parental authority and magnification of fears over possible separation from the security of home. Within the peer groups, too — and as an offshoot of the educational propensity to grade kids on the outcome of superiority struggles — children have to compete among themselves to gain standing: to resent others for being "better," to deprecate oneself for not being "best," and to scorn those lower in the pecking order. The easy bottom of any such order is the brain-handicapped child.

Even in the matter of childhood guilt there are exceptional circumstances prevalent today. Prolonged guilt, often for nothing more than an imagined wrong, may impair speech and learning. Fair punishment relieves guilt. It is also as much a part of love as praise. Yet theories of child-raising psychologically equated destructive behavior with healthy release, or "letting it all out." If a kid in rage kicked parents, they were supposed to approve the act as honest and satisfying. Little cognizance was taken of the fact that the child still might negatively express feelings and be very helpfully disciplined for it. Unfair punishment is only unfairness, but when there is *no* discipline administered by those who care, life has a way of meting out punishments of its own as the child pushes for needed limits and, finding none, slips over the line into amoral behavior.

The reality and management of childhood anger are also little understood. Among adults, anger is suppressed as wrong, and constructive expressions of it are too rarely seen by children — only the extremes, actual or dramatized, which further endorse negative attitudes about anger, while letting pass as acceptable the daily petty meanness that creates more anger. Parents who try to bottle up anger often succeed only in displacing it — externally on the wrong persons, internally in a variety of depressive ailments. Children caught in the indifference of the classroom learn the fine art of "cool" while venting their anger in problem behavior. There are many constructive ways of expressing anger. None includes gratuitous physical or verbal assaults. All begin with identifying the source and accepting simple anger.

While childhood doubt may become exaggerated through attempts to participate in the extended peer group without being exposed as inadequate, the total fabric of adult society does little to relieve deep feelings of personal shame that many children experience. When adults are preoccupied with social appearances and fears of losing face, their children sense that if they somehow come off on the short end of things, they had best conceal and not talk about it at home, had best keep their mouths shut, misplace the poor report card, turn on television to forget having been jeered at as the brother or sister of a "retard," swallow tears so as not to be called a crybaby, mention successes only, act proud when there is little to be proud about — put up the good front they know to be a sham.

Sexually, every child is identified as being either a

boy or a girl. Mother is female, father is male. These sex identifications are made every day, in every type of situation, with or without a concomitant sense of desire but always with the knowledge that such differences have a genital basis. It is natural for a child to want to know why one is a "he" or a "she" and not an "it," what makes this so and how is it to be used. Moreover, every child grows through stages of sexual gratification — in Freudian terms, oral, anal, genital, homosexual, heterosexual. To expect that this area of growth, so fundamental to all human identity, can be achieved in the absence of adult explanation, with harsh reproval for curiosity, is as foolish as expecting youngsters to learn manners from cattle. Such an unwise expectation is further compounded by the fact that the adult world uses sex as a vehicle for selling goods and services, so it is everywhere apparent that arrival at puberty has a lot of competitive status, even if one doesn't know what to do with it and is taught to control feelings.

Only when parents recognize the ordinary and extraordinary problems of growing up can they intelligently take steps to relieve undue stress in their children. Open talk within the family is *the* most important way to counter peer-group pressures and ambivalent social values — open talk including discussion of real feelings and honest, understandable answers to questions as they arise. Asking questions is a learning process for youngsters that reveals their thinking and needs. Some questions, of course, may have no finite answer, in which case the truth is, "I don't know," not "Don't ask stupid things." Others aren't meant for any answer at all apart from affectionate endorsement, as with the oft-repeated "When are we going to get there?" during a trip. But if a four-year-old asks, "Where do babies come from?" anything short of the simple, unembarrassed truth is an evasion — *and the child knows it.* From the first, the attempt at honesty establishes open talk in the family and trust in the parents as the source of reliable information, regardless of external pressures. This is a two-way street, for parents also learn what are the real concerns of their children, and the joy of dynamic conversation grows from that point, as each year the questions from an expanding mind gain greater sophistication.

The effort to define truth simplifies communication about a developmental disability. One of the first wonderments a youngster expresses when a brother or sister has a brain handicap is whether the sibling is sick. Any reasonable answer means trying to explain injury to the unseen brain. Subsequent questions may include: Does it hurt? Will it get better? If these questions are brushed aside, the subject becomes something not to be talked about — an unmentionable that arouses fear and reinforces peer-group ignorance.

Open talk, whatever the pitfalls, is the pathway to understanding, the preface to knowledgeable compassion. Any child can accept the fact that parents are worried when they admit they are. In that acceptance, the child also feels intuitively reassured, aware that just as mother and father make exceptional efforts for the afflicted one, they would do the same for each person in the family — *because* they love, *because* they care, because they *aren't kidding themselves.* Evasion signifies indifference or unmanageable anxiety. Knowing means trying, and there is no child on earth who isn't ready to try, all the way, to help loving parents. Additionally, an informed child is armed with truth outside the home, more secure in a basic trust of home, while an uninformed child is essentially bewildered and therefore vulnerable to misinformation.

When parents can speak freely about brain handicap, so can the child, equipped with the facts and, more importantly, knowing that there is nothing to be ashamed about. Instead of feeling victimized by circumstance, the youngster learns to become an initiator — which is one of the healthiest uses of natural aggression — and sees that trying to make others like ourselves is a hostile act, denying one's own expression of love and denying others the right to be themselves.

In any family, the evolution of open talk goes through three stages: elemental, sophisticated, contributory. Simple questions with clear answers are the basis for all subsequent elaboration, until the time is reached when the child becomes an important *source* of new information. Honestly informed, the contributory youngster is alert to out-of-home advice that might help — things that others facing similar situations have found useful, an ally in an allied family, a partisan among caring partisans. Instead of being wounded by adversity, the developing mind has learned perhaps the most vital task of life: to see things as they *are*, not as a bull duped into charging the matador's cape.

Most relations of any sort break down in the absence of communications. When a family has a developmentally disabled child, the importance of openness, as a first priority, thus cannot be overestimated. However, if it is true that man cannot live by bread alone, it is equally true that we cannot live on talk alone, either. We need to join in necessary tasks, and the quality of talk is improved by many activities, from work to recreation. At home, all begin with sharing chores: sweeping, dusting, washing dishes, making beds, setting the table and so on. Pitching in on the work is a direct way of expressing, "We are a family and proud of it." Each tries to do what is possible, including the brain-handicapped child. Some concept of routine that sets forth what needs to be done, by whom and when, can also be useful, giving shape and organization to the day in order to clear away chores as a preface to enjoying other things.

Along with sharing work comes the responsibility of learning to share and manage money. When money is held to be the parents' business, children are denied the chance to understand its source, its limitations and its uses. Money becomes a handout available through entreaty, not something to be earned and wisely spent. If parents pool income, it ceases to be "his" or "hers," and the sense of "ours" prevails. But what is "ours" to the parents should extend to the children, too. Of course, most family funds have to be applied collectively in paying bills and buying groceries. Yet if it's fair for Mom and Dad to have a little private spending money, the same is fair for kids — an allowance not as a gratuity but as *earned* family salary. When it's gone, it's gone, until next payday. This teaches relative values to youngsters, handicapped or not, as well as the ways of helping out when one person is in need and the other has more.

A good pet can also be a great teacher and an added dimension of joy. It is of special significance to the family with a developmental disability. Pets take love and care, are physically different but nonetheless capable of giving and receiving affection, of communicating without words. There are wide areas of human learning in relation to a pet. These include all aspects of basic existence — training, feeding, belonging, a place to sleep, health care.

With or without an animal, every home benefits from raising household plants. Children learn the simple art of watering and cultivating, becoming caretakers of a silent companion. They also see what good and bad care can do to any living thing.

Setting goals is something parents do, but it unites a family to discuss and agree upon them. When parents simply tell kids, "This must be done," doing it is begrudged as an obligation. But if kids are asked, "What do you think about this?" the direction is into the realm of advice and consent, through which children learn the essentials of setting goals and making the plans by which to meet them. This does not mean leaning on children as crutches, leaving decisions up to them beyond their abilities. It means including and guiding them — and ofttimes learning from them.

There are so many inexpensive and invaluable recreational activities open to a family that it is impossible to place qualitative rankings on any. Games, picnics, camp-

ing, singing, bedtime stories — each family has to decide
what is most rewarding to it, in terms of its collective
character and readiness to try new things. Whatever the
means, it can be said that all work and no play doesn't
just make Jack a dull boy, it reduces life to a drag of
acute proportions that no family can withstand, let alone
a family with a developmentally disabled youngster.

When parents are in doubt about sibling stress, some
clues to its presence may come from listening to dreams.
Of course, we've all observed that there are those who
listen but don't seem to hear, and others who hear but
don't seem to listen. So it is necessary to hearken atten-
tively, for through dreams the brain endeavors to relieve
tangled feelings and sort things out. The interpretation
of dreams may be speculative, though fascinating; the
emotions involved are definitely not speculative, and listening is a way of letting them be uttered and accepted,
to avoid turning a dream of the night into a fear of the
day. Children go through all the moods parents do, only
lack adult perspective. Under stress, dreams (often symbolic) reveal troubled thoughts related to identity, guilt,
anger, doubt and sexuality. These can tell parents many
things about their children's inner struggles, help them
know and try to understand.

In every family, to achieve open talk, to determine
the character of work and play, to perceive spoken and
unspoken needs, some leadership is required, or else
everything breaks down in conflict. Socially we tend to
equate authority with rank and power, but it is indeed
true that he who is servant of all is master of all. It isn't

a matter of whether Dad is the boss or Mom wears the pants, for real leadership has nothing to do with dictating. Troops may be coerced by the exercise of superior power, but troops led are those who would voluntarily lay down their lives for someone who stands for the common good and well-being of all. So true leadership in the family means sitting down in council and letting needs be known first before attempting to propose answers to them.

To hearken to the concerns of the child and honor them is to be hearkened to *and* honored. In the battle to understand ourselves and others, there is no greater honor.

▣ Education

IT IS WIDELY ACKNOWLEDGED THAT ALL CHILDREN have the right to formal education. In the United States, they *must* have it, starting at ever more early ages, whether they or their parents want it. Regardless of what kind of job the public schools do, parents still have to pay the mushrooming costs for them through property taxes. This levy is not just for the years their children are enrolled but for the life of the property, with no deduction for electing the alternate of private school. Since state and federal governments also contribute, the obligatory program is enormously and increasingly expensive, without the financial reality of competition.

Meanwhile, courts endeavor to use schools to rectify real and present social iniquities; parent groups argue over the inclusion or exclusion of various extracurricular activities; the deluge of regulations gags administration; and staffing innovations rise like dinosaurs in a swamp, as the salesmen come and go, speaking of teaching tools. Proven texts are phased out for the latest passing concept, arithmetic is set aside for new math, word grouping takes the place of learning to read, and fine old buildings are torn down for replacement by an architectural box admired as better because it may attract industry.

On this perennial battlefield, children are supposed to study, have their lives enriched, come out whole, sane and motivated, find a niche in society, and cherish memories of the experience. Twenty-three percent don't graduate; twenty percent graduate functionally illiterate, draped in gowns from the sixteenth century, unable to read signs or make change.

Most brain handicap — in particular, mild retardation, epilepsy and MBD — does not show up until after children enter this mind mill. Since mental disorders appear to be on the rise, we must review both the direct and indirect reasons in an effort to improve learning. Schools are not spontaneous creations. They reflect surrounding communities, physically and academically — are symptoms rather than causes of behavioral patterns. It is shortsighted to look only at the end result while neglecting all else.

No matter what a child faces outside home, the way in which it is faced derives from experiences *at* home. Lack of warm care, which can lead to so many difficulties, may stem from the view that motherhood is menial, homemaking a form of drudgery. Men have helped further this notion through a system of acclaim for out-of-home achievements and second-class status for women and domestic skills. Thus it is considered important to be a celebrity, unimportant to prepare a good meal; important to make money, unimportant to do creative housekeeping and make best use of the household budget. Such concepts have stimulated an industry of conveniences — the instant meals and host of appliances to minimize housework so one can be free to engage in socially applauded tasks. We have also created a value system in which displaying the externals of success has significance, while talking with one's child seems a bother. On December 11, 1976, ABC-TV news reported that in national surveys ninety-seven percent of seventeen-year-old girls said they did not wish to become housewives. Implicit in such a view may be the feeling that it is desirable or more stimulating to compete in the masculine arena and that there is something inherently tedious about loving children and managing a home.

The extraordinary power of a woman is not masculine, thank God, and anything that denies it takes away from the essence of womanhood. Femininity is by no means degrading, unless through doubt one believes it to be so, submitting to sexist role expectations; or, if money is the measure of self-worth, the Internal Revenue Service reports that of the 38,000 American millionaires, only 11,000 are men. Certainly women — and men — must be liberated, but *not* at the expense of children. Isn't a more truthful definition of freedom to be found in the act of making glad the beginnings of a someday adult, liberating both male *and* female from the emotional bondage of parental indifference?

When home is regarded as a place of captivity, tasks in it seem to take on some semblance of chain-gang labor. This may prove rancorous in general. It can be disastrous in many particulars. Nutrition is the most obvious example. Every growing child continues to need a well-balanced diet. Without it, there is risk of impairing mental capacity. As Dr. Myron Winick has found in *Malnutrition and Brain Development*, malnourished infants tend to develop poorly and may become intellectually retarded. Since most brain handicap shows up after the start of school years, we should look closely at the possible causal relation between deficient eating habits and the emergence of a mental disability.

We have already discussed the importance of stimulation in nursing, whether by breast or by bottle, and the baby's need to receive an adequate spectrum of nutrients. If the nursing process is hastened as something to be gotten out of the way as soon as possible, to what extent does that haste contribute to the formation of later attitudes toward meals in general, with increasing reference to and overuse of speed foods to cut time spent cooking and eating during the child's developmental years? Some artificial colors to make these foods look good have already been banned. Others are in doubt. None has been scrutinized in terms of its affect on the growing brain, though physicians such as Benjamin F. Feingold of the Kaiser Medical Center in San Francisco believe that some are involved in certain cases of MBD. "Fast foods" are heavily refined, with lost nutritional values replaced by insignificant additives. Most rely on sweeteners and other sales-oriented flavorings. Families can get full on tasty, attractive nothingness, with the impoverished system later demanding an equally deficient between-meals snack.

It is not just a woman's job to understand the basics of proper nutrition, it is also a man's — to help improve the market by not spending money on unwise items, and to help restore pride in the creative art of preparing balanced meals. Feeding children junk and expecting them to go to school mentally alert and physically strong makes no sense. Nor will parents do well on days when they have consumed inadequate food in a hurry under tension. What can a child learn in class if body and mind are expressing needs created at the breakfast table but construed as social and educational irritants? Learning is growing, and growing is learning. Children don't have to be pushed to do either. They *can't* do either without sound nutrition. Yet as Merrill S. Read of the National Institute of Child Health notes in the October 1973 issue of the *Journal of the American Dietetic Association*, an estimated twenty-five percent of American children arrive at school on an empty stomach. Quite possibly an even higher number arrive improperly fed.

Today, the thrust is toward school enrollment at an increasingly earlier age. But no day-care center or school can replace parents who have pride in their home life, and the act of sending a child away too soon may be viewed by the child as rejection. The cult of early achievement, coupled with premature exile, tends to place enormous pressure on youngsters to excel before they comprehend why and for what. Children have different degrees of readiness. Though each needs social interaction, especially after age five, all have a better chance to evolve in the security of home than in the newness of school until balanced development, not an arbitrary age, is reached. That is, they should attain sufficient mental, physical *and* emotional confidence first before being expected to do their best at or benefit from formal education. In some cases, this may occur rather early, and such children, with adult guidance and evaluation, should not necessarily be held back. In others, the child may need extra time, without pushing, to achieve the right stage of readiness. All this suggests is that educationally we appear to have an opportunity to advance the mental well-being of children through more attention to the individual and less to standardized points of departure.

When youngsters are sent from home before they are able to handle out-of-home instruction, they may experience elevated emotions while their brains are still rapidly growing. To what extent this relates to the high incidence of mental disabilities appearing after the start of school is uncertain. But surely we must appreciate the connection between the evident behavioral and perceptual problems that emerge and the intensity of what the child feels, expected to achieve in a strange environment, under a physically confining program of brain-training that encourages conformity to sameness as it rewards efforts to be better than others and reprimands failures.

To such an environment, parents can unintentionally bring added pressures through natural though unrealistic overambitions for their child, academically, athletically or socially. Thus, some parents may want greater emphasis placed on winning teams in the major sports and exhort their kids to go all out, unaware of the potential untoward physical and emotional demands this exacts of formative youngsters, or the possible detriment to their academic and behavioral learning. Since only those able to compete in such sports are eligible, the emphasis also tends to reduce needed sporting opportunities for the developmentally disabled. Yet other parents may incline to want the faculty to advance their children faster than is advised for best development, or require teachers to correct home-based problems with discipline instead of teaching skills that help the kids to overcome them. Under these circumstances, youngsters are often placed in the stressful position of acting as go-betweens for adults, exercising the daily shuttle diplomacy of trying to please parents and teachers at the same time, while not being accused of subservience by their peers. If grown-ups can experience the mental disability of nervous breakdowns, what about kids?

As a constant condition of the school environment, there is the influence of the social and physical environment. Polluted air and water are known to be disease-producing, but few studies have examined their potential adverse effects on the developing brain. Also, we recognize the tension brought about in adults by an achievement-oriented society that caters to the myth of the well-adjusted person while discussing the balance of terror as if it were another ordinary conversational subject; but have we asked ourselves how, under this same tension, children are to grow up mentally sound? Though we each sustain some developmental wounds, today the chances of their becoming serious are not only one in ten but rising.

Until recently, brain handicap was little understood by schools. The afflicted were not considered educable, an opinion supported by the community, and so they remained at home, except for those with concealed epilepsy and others who could manage to fill the spot at the bottom of the class — meaning, education was mandatory for everyone *except* those most in need. However, with the passage of new laws, schools were obliged to serve the developmentally disabled and opened programs of special education. This was good, but in principle and in practice it segregated into separate rooms and groups anyone unable to fit into regular classes, the philosophy of categorizing being an offshoot of segregating children according to age, the way it was earlier fashionable to segregate according to sex.

Exposure to brain handicap accomplished several things: (1) a sudden awareness of the magnitude of the problem, which was greater than researchers had anticipated; (2) attempts to devise screening materials to identify deviants; and (3) the systematic reference to medication as a teaching aid. From the total ignorance of the 1950s, education moved in twenty years to the other extreme of viewing almost every behavioral difference as a disability that could be handled with a pill. Simultaneously, the post-Sputnik panic about falling behind in education led to an unsound, unplanned and unwise rush to expand curriculums, making school an increasingly serious business for kids and elevating behavioral problems.

It is of course necessary to spot the early signs of learning difficulty to prevent emotional trauma when a child can't keep up, both in class and at home, and is punished in various ways for the incapability. With brain handicap, performance isn't improved by keeping the youngster after school, adding extra homework or issuing complaints to worried parents. Such demands only create more anxieties, which further reduce performance.

Among the now recognized learning disabilities are: hyperactivity, minimal brain dysfunction, dyslexia and, of late, the dyslogic syndrome, or brain inability to compute. Early signs are poor handwriting, printing letters backward, word confusion and physical awkwardness. However, there is a maze of conflicting professional advice about these disabilities, including the statistical folklore that attempts to explain most juvenile delinquency in terms of learning disabilities, and this has given rise to a host of screening materials to determine who has a mental handicap and who doesn't.

Every child entering school takes a battery of standardized tests designed to measure unmeasurable qualities. Many, of course, can be useful. But some may invade the privacy of the home; others can subject the student to the worry of undue scrutiny; a few are for the convenience of faculty doctoral dissertations, or are fostered by agencies selling remedial devices. None can *substitute* for the teacher's in-class perception, which should be shared with the parents, just as they need to share their information with the teacher. Yet most tests have the potential to provide a simplistic technical label that becomes part of the permanent record, passed on with the child from grade to grade. The next teacher is thus led to expect a problem and may pay more attention to the record than to the reality; or if the teacher happens to see that preceding teachers misjudged, any observation to that effect may be couched in a manner that won't jeopardize professional standing among them. Sometimes the substance of the record sticks with the child outside the classroom and prefaces what the child tries to do elsewhere, in work or recreation. Labels tend to be self-fulfilling prophesies, and an early label is often tantamount to the pronouncement of sentence, without right of appeal. All behavior becomes suspect until proved otherwise.

When behavior is simplified to fit the label, any behavior outside of that label is usually seen as an exception rather than as a possible behavior change. Every label is also highly interpretive. Under one set of circumstances, for example, a student may be termed passive for not fighting back, antisocial for preferring to eat lunch alone, noncommunicative for befriending pigeons. The labels, not the qualifiers, are then picked up along the line, and if the student seems uncooperative and difficult to handle because of being misperceived, the attempt is to go ahead and normalize the child in some program, normal school being for the normal, even though no two people fit a specific norm.

Once some kind of disability is suspected, the all-too-common recourse is to prescribe drugs to correct it. With no clear guidelines to the contrary, a natural extension of the pill-for-all-ills syndrome is the effort to "cure" behavior, medicating the pupil who cannot get along with the teacher. Instead of looking at what school may be doing wrong to children, it becomes easier to blame the problem on a learning disability and tranquilize the student. The right of every child entering school should be the right to *no* treatment, the right *not* to be screened, unless or until other legitimate avenues of care prove unavailing.

Medication to treat the brain has a primary effect, a set of secondary or side effects, and a variable withdrawal symptom. For instance, amphetamine therapy for hyperactivity may in certain cases be followed by profound depression when the medication is withdrawn. It may also create high dopamine levels in the brain. (As Hugh Brown of the University of Miami has determined, one clinical feature of schizophrenia is elevated brain dopamine.) Other pills dampen rather than resolve emotional conflicts, and withdrawal is accompanied by deep feelings of fear. Children need to be taught how to cope with frustrations in order to learn that the business of life isn't the absence of problems but how one attempts to solve them. Casual medication precludes that process, blunting sensations, altering the neuro-hormonal transmitters needed for thought. Mellow behavior in the classroom is then held to be constructive, and the teacher writes glowing reports of progress. After legally taking uppers and downers for twelve or more years of school, what does the child take when released to society from the hallowed halls of learning? The ambiguity of the legal process here is that on the one hand it jails kids for street drugs and, on the other, pushes them in schools for those who don't meet arbitrary standards.

The entire concept of special education itself has distinct limitations. It is based on the notion that fast learners are inconvenienced by slow learners, and that slow learners are better off when set apart to plod along. This may have validity in the abstract, but where do we draw the line between fast and slow learning? What about children whose performance varies from year to year? Do we put kids into advanced class one year and drop them back the next if they can't keep up? And if kids are stuck into a reduced niche, is the system capable of recognizing their ability to get out of it?

Special education segregates developmentally disabled children from the wider horizons of regular class and restricts their needed experience of variety by obliging them to associate only with other handicapped persons instead of learning how to get about in society at large. It also precludes those who are not developmentally disabled from direct contact with brain handicap. The idea behind grouping youngsters according to achievement levels may be that it aids the detection and stimulation of superior intellect. Fail-rate of such child prodigies in life adjustment is often very high, the child essentially having learned what pleases adults, sometimes to the exclusion of *self*-discovery. Most real genius goes through school without ever being identified, since growth rates change, there are many other types of "genius" than can be expressed in academic work, and computer testing is unable to measure such qualities as creativity or original thought. Nor does intelligence necessarily have much to do with "scholastic aptitude" and the rapid tabulation of trifles. At the risk of oversimplifying, perhaps we can say that IQ is a matter of trying to outsmart someone else, while intelligence is the realization that you can outsmart yourself.

The myth of superiority is equally damaging to inter-personal relations, all voluntary behavior — including emotional — being *learned*. The myth further assumes standards of normality and abnormality that cannot be precisely defined. Isn't genius abnormal? Perhaps we should have "normalized" Einstein. After all, he had an early speech problem. If there are acceptable and un-acceptable kinds of abnormality, society might do well to recognize that it cannot begin to understand genius until it begins to understand the developmentally dis-abled. Over the ages, societies that have rejected their brain-handicapped have tended to martyr their greatest contributors; and those who have accepted the brain-handicapped with compassion have more readily honored their greatest contributors. When differences are taught to be feared, the uniform drive is to succeed through con-formity and to deny, deprive or eliminate anyone who does not fit the standard.

Before schools recommend treatment for a suspected brain handicap, the child should first be tested for vision, hearing, perception, gross- and fine-motor de-velopment, as well as for other physical, emotional or nutritional problems. If children can't see the blackboard from the front row, how are they going to learn what's written on it? If children can't hear instruction, how are they going to comprehend and answer a question? If children have difficulty holding a pencil, how are they to use it? If they're under stress at home, how can they approach any test with relaxed confidence? But time and again, children are bewildered by requests to answer what they cannot see, are considered inattentive if they didn't hear instruction, deemed deficient if the hand can't manage the pencil, proclaimed backward if worry about parents has greater meaning than a piece of paper asking them to make sense of an arrangement of numbers. Sometimes, obvious eye and ear problems can go undetected through the fifth grade; and an IQ test taken at age nine — let us say, under personal duress at home and a hostile teacher at school — is held to be conclusive throughout the remaining years of education. Too many unkind judgments are passed on little children by adults who are loudest to protest any infringement against them of the tenet: judge not that ye be not judged. "Look for flaws," an old Hindu proverb goes, "see no people."

Often such judgments are based on testing error and lead to remedial courses of action where none was necessary. In every class, there is usually one pupil who seems harder to teach than the others and is therefore viewed as the source of all problems, which, if removed, would resolve everything. Special education offers the easy out, not necessarily the best way. Under the guise of helping a brain-handicapped youngster, the school transfers the person to a room filled with other presumed difficulties, there to learn how to raise mayhem. Some in the group may be autistic or retarded and suffer seriously; others may have epilepsy or cerebral palsy and wonder if they are being punished. If we could say that these errors benefited the majority of pupils, there might be some justification for the system, but that is infrequently the case. Many schools seem to be doing a far better job of demoralizing kids than educating them, and one origin of that demoralization is the ready option to banish those who inconvenience the teacher: the label will get you if you don't watch out.

A poor teacher is a monolithic structure of set ways that tend to create continuing difficulties for other members of the faculty. But a good teacher is flexible in method and teaches understanding by *being* understanding, is just, has no "pet" or "whipping boy," observes and can give individual praise, as well as help ease a student over a rough spot. It may be rare to find one, but when you do, you never forget the experience.

For every acknowledged mode of instruction, there are usually several workable alternates. The question is not *how* something is taught but *if* it is getting across. To insist on unchangeable means when a child is not learning to read, write and count is nonsensical — as nonsensical as sitting stubbornly behind the dignity of a desk and calling for order when all the interesting education is going on at the other end of the room. Finding the way to get instruction across is what teaching is all about, what makes it a paid profession, not a custodial pastime. This may be harder to do with the brain-handicapped, but in the challenge lie the seeds of care from which the class learns the very meaning of care. It can be a revelation to discover that two and two are four not because we say so but because we have symbols to describe quantities for a purpose. Unless the purpose is clear, the addition of quantities remains incomprehensible. A child's perception of that purpose doesn't necessarily come about by grouping objects, unless the objects and the grouping are desired.

What is desired and what isn't also reveals something about the child. The teacher's effort to get through, with patience and goodwill, teaches patience and goodwill, and others in the class readily help out, rather than learning to despise the slow learner and, in the act of despising, learn to fear becoming one. In a constructive spirit, too, children offer many useful insights that ease the task of teaching — such as pointing out that one pupil may not grasp the addition of two oranges and two oranges because the pupil, for whatever reason, doesn't know what an orange is.

The same applies to the teaching of reading and writing. We have agreed upon a code of symbols to represent sounds that make up words which, when connected, convey thought. The standard philosophy is to begin with the simple and proceed to the complex. But learning to spell "cat" is of little significance to someone who dislikes or isn't interested in cats; having to memorize the alphabet is irrelevant in the absence of some purpose for it; and children who have confronted all manner of complexities in and around home — from death to riots — may not see the simple as having much to do with the real. Force-feeding pap to children is a singularly unnourishing enterprise. Frustration and boredom in class often cause aggression outside it. When a kid is passed on from one grade to another without having learned anything useful, the process simply isn't education. As educator Leslie A. Hart states in *How the Brain*

Works, "The typical classroom, based on captivity and incessant threat, can hardly be surpassed as a counterproductive environment." But when reading and writing are directly related to learning and using basic skills, and children are not *told* what to think but allowed to discover, school becomes exciting. The developmentally disabled child, in such a class, gains greatly. So do classmates who are encouraged to understand and assist.

In practically every area of instruction, teaching the emotional and social aspects of development as well as conventional academic subjects has special importance. In this, American education has generally been negligent. The brain-handicapped child needs to know not just about numbers and words but about appearance, discipline, manners, health, fitness, affection, work, homemaking, dating and sex. So do we all. Kids want to get along as best they can. Yet the crucial, learned tasks of behavior are often held to be not part of the classroom beyond primary grades.

They are — most intimately. For school, unlike independent studies or private instruction, is a social experience, and the quality of what is learned in class is a direct function of how the class is conducted and how classmates interrelate. Laying down discipline without teaching the value of discipline simply exercises abstract authority. Stipulating anything behavioral without teaching values invites lack of interest in academic tasks. How do we get along with others? help at home? settle disagreements? solve problems? earn money? keep healthy? make friends? know love? What *is* happiness? What is our own unique meaning, and how do we find it? Personal fulfillment begins with accepting our shared humanity, regardless of the degree of brain advantage or disadvantage.

The individual character of each brain defies standardized instruction, and rote memorizing has little to do with development. Instead, we need more emphasis on variety and inventiveness. Since children's minds have a lot of growing to do, it is important that the child not become molded too soon. Each should be inspired to try for answers, not fear that something is personally wrong if the answer is incorrect. All learning is for survival. So in addition to humanizing our schools, perhaps we could look to changing the basis of education to five-step, problem-oriented instruction: (1) defining the problem; (2) conceiving responses to it; (3) selecting the best answer; (4) putting the answer to work; and (5) evaluating the result. Subjects would thus be taught not so much as abstracts (although the development of abstract thought should be encouraged) as informational tools to be used in planning and executing answers to realistic problems, the problems increasing in complexity as the child is able to manage greater complexities. Since there is an evident distinction between what we call cleverness and what we call wisdom, I also feel that we could try to place more *equal* emphasis on the four basic areas of communication: verbal, artistic, musical and physical. In too many schools, expression through art, music and dance is held to be extracurricular beyond the early grades.

Parents can help themselves and their child greatly by making a friend of the teacher so that the relation between home and school is better understood, not polarized. If every child has a right to education, every parent and teacher has an obligation to make the most of it, not expect the effort to succeed when the only communication is conflict or, conversely, meaningless niceties — as happens when PTAs and school boards are not representative. Schools can't make up for omissions at home, nor can home make up for educational ineptitude. A cooperative relation begins on a one-to-one basis — through the attempt to understand and grow in wisdom. This is, after all, the essence of education.

◼ Adolescence

TO LOVE AND BE LOVED, TO BE OPEN TO FEELING, TO have the right of sexual expression is indispensable to the growth and maturation of all. It is particularly important to the development of those we call developmentally disabled. Yet perhaps because the disabled tend to be misperceived, our taboos about sex are often more strictly enforced upon them. So while many may agree that they should somehow manage to be as "normal" as possible in most regards, they are nonetheless commonly expected to remain asexual — at home, in school, in institutions or in society at large.

Programs for the mentally retarded abound — special education, activity centers, work training, residential services, and so forth. There is infant stimulation, early intervention, mainstreaming, normalization, remediation, vocational rehabilitation, job placement, and all the polysyllabic rest of it. But in a land where condoms, diaphragms and the pill are in wide use and advertised, the notion of making contraception instruction and contraceptive devices available to the retarded is usually viewed with disapproval. And at a time when young people cohabit, or publicly greet each other with affection, the thought of such behavior between the brain-handicapped is considered unacceptable, as though they would *never* be able to "handle" that area of life properly.

In the main, it seems that society has refused to discuss, let alone decide, whether sex is a right or a privilege. It cannot be both. A privilege is something bestowed by others. A right is what each of us is entitled to without discrimination. Thus, one is elected into a club as a privilege but enrolled in school as a right. Both rights and privileges offer us benefits and demand of us certain obligations and responsibilities. If sexual expression is a privilege, who grants it? What are the rules? But if sexual expression is a right, then isn't everyone entitled to enjoy that right unprejudicially? Even if we say that sex is a right for some and not for others, based on certain criteria, who decides *what* criteria should preface validation of the right?

There are countless ambiguities that have not been answered with regard to sex and the developmentally disabled. Informally, it appears that sexual expression under various circumstances should be curbed, and that it is desirable for some individuals to live sexually constrained or segregated. But let us consider the latter more closely: if we call people of the same sex "homosexual" for joining together, are we saying that society favors enforced homosexuality in cases where policy requires people to be segregated according to sex? Moreover, at what point do we begin with sexual segregation? — at birth? during childhood? in adolescence? If at birth, then it follows that boy babies should sleep only with their fathers and girl babies only with their mothers. If during childhood, then every activity from play to sleep, not just in the bathroom, has to occur under sexually separate circumstances. Or if in adolescence, what of the effect on someone who has enjoyed heterosexual relations — eating, talking and being in a mixed group — up to that point? How would any of us feel if, with all the intense new feelings of puberty, we were suddenly removed from the mainstream of social interaction?

Sexuality doesn't begin at maturation. It begins before birth in the balance of hormones to the fetus and develops from birth through the infancy affection between mother and child, the pleasures of sucking, being fondled, wiped and changed — an affection profound enough to make some fathers feel jealous of a new son unless they take an active part in giving affection, too. This psychosexual development, so vital to growth of love for ourselves and others, proceeds through stages: attachment to the security blanket, anal satisfactions, discovery of sex play, masturbation, touching and showing, homosexuality, impersonation, finally at puberty involving the tumultuous urgings of hormonal changes and the social realization that it is all right for boys to befriend boys and girls to befriend girls, but not for members of the same sex to fondle each other, and that one desires and is desirable to the opposite sex, yet cannot altogether figure out what to do about it.

Full sexual maturation is not a simple matter of organs and their physical enlargement. It encompasses the *learned* history of sensual experience and the evolution from one stage to another. This development is as important to the brain-handicapped child as it is to anyone else, yet it is made more complicated for the very one who could use some helpful simplification. Because such youngsters tend to be more closely watched, they may be punished for sex play that passes unnoticed among their peers. Even if they are not under constant surveillance, they often lack strategies of concealment, making their actions more obvious than those of others. Adult instruction, not blame and punishment, should be the response. Yet adults embarrassed about their own sexuality may fail the brain-handicapped child to a greater degree than they do their other children. Being set apart from peers at school further adds to the youngster's difficulty in establishing interpersonal relations. Sometimes these children may be led into, or become the object of, sex games, with the primary intent of leaving them exposed to the teacher's shock. Sometimes their behavior is simply more overt owing to reduced alertness to imminent detection.

In the process of groping for self-definition and defending against ridicule, a child can become deeply confused about sexual identity. Many disabled young boys may see themselves only in their mothers' roles, and arrival at adolescence is not just a crisis but an unmitigated anguish. If a brain-handicapped teenage girl, seeking approval and affection, is induced into the bushes by a boy who fears to pursue more self-reliant girls, she is the one held up to be the problem, not the boy who made the "easy score." Or if a brain-handicapped teenage boy is led on by his peers, through the guise of gaining their approval, to pull down the pants of a girl publicly because the others wanted to get a look but were afraid, he's the culprit, the sexually uncontrolled one, not those who took advantage of his gullibility.

An appalling amount of misinformation clouds our understanding and management of the sexuality of the brain-handicapped adolescent, who is nonetheless supposed to display behavior and attain psychosexual development difficult enough for the nondisabled. We know that sexuality is profoundly influenced by segregated institutionalization, whether in prison or in mental hospitals. Indeed, it is sometimes influenced by cloistering men together for long periods in military or religious confines, or by sending youngsters to all-boy, all-girl boarding schools. But when a developmentally disabled teenager is asked to perform in society, while restrained from expressing affection, kept away from dances and other mixed social events, the effect is perhaps more serious than what happens in institutions, since the evidence of what is being denied is so obvious.

Coupled with social ignorance about sex is the fact that acceptable instruction about it usually carries an overload of medical words and evasions. To introduce a course on sex education, for instance, schools are often advised to conduct prudent surveys first. If the course is approved, sometimes resulting classes are sexually separate and communications couched in sonorous terminology. So it is apparent from the first that what is being taught is quite unlike any other subject — often to the point of having little to do with student reality. Certainly, a young man who has gone through a pack of condoms isn't much interested in being told about wet dreams, any more than a young woman on the pill is going to find a discussion of menstruation especially informative.

The primary concern of any adolescent is not to be told the Latin words for already known and used sex organs, or to be shown medical cutaways of bodies more fascinatingly pictured in magazines, but to know: (1) what makes one adequate and attractive to the opposite sex; (2) how loving relates to the giving and receiving of pleasure; (3) how two people may recognize the difference between temporary desire and long-range fulfillment; and (4) what marriage and parenting involve. Such knowledge cannot be expected to come automatically, or through adult example that remains private. Nor is it best acquired through informal trial and error. Above all, the need is to eliminate fear of sex — fear of inadequacy, performance demands and taboos.

Of course, some parents may fear and therefore object to frank, finite and coeducational discussion of sex. But in the absence of it, teenagers learn what is publicly available: that pleasing a man is a matter of what looks good in a bikini, that pleasing a woman comes from being endowed with all that money can buy, that love is a commodity or multiple orgasm, that desire is a function of the youthful figure. What this does to people when youth has passed is everywhere apparent in the middle-aged failure of relations, the sadly troubled concerns over the natural and inevitable erosions of time.

To the developmentally disabled, lacking competitive physical and social attributes, it further confuses an already confused attempt at gender identification. Still, we hear about programs for "normalization" of the brain-handicapped in almost every area *but* sex: "normalized" to live in the community, not "normalized" to love in the community; "normalized" to work in the community, not "normalized" to be married in the community; "normalized" to be taught homemaking, not "normalized" to be taught about sexual needs; "normalized" to wash the genitals but not to have any feeling in them; "normalized" to look attractive but not to the opposite sex. Of course, normalization may have different implications for different people. Regardless of the implications, however, such concepts and the formal programs that grow out of them are suspect unless they include instruction on sexual identity, expression, contraception and hygiene.

Despite the fact that community attitudes toward sex and the brain-handicapped reflect attitudes toward brain handicap in general, this instruction has to be available at home, through schools, and in activity or residential centers on a coeducational basis. Otherwise, it is impossible to expect the individual to develop without serious emotional deficits or, just as important, to learn acceptable behavior publicly and privately. Enforcing "control" accomplishes neither, the repressed drive being channeled into other less desirable forms of self-gratification.

All sex education should be based on the four primary aspects of function: (1) the act of love as being the most intimate form of mutual rapture between two people who have found continuing pleasure in each other's company before engaging in sexual intercourse; (2) the fundamentals of contraception; (3) prevention or avoidance of venereal infections; and (4) relationships in living together. Every maturing child has to be counseled in these matters, by parents and teachers. If parents do their job, the teacher's job would be far easier. It may seem more difficult, because of the need for explicit description, to explain sexual functions to someone with a brain handicap. But except in extreme cases, it is generally an attainable objective.

Far from encouraging kids to go out and participate in orgies — the unfounded fear of some adults — honest, accurate and complete sexual guidance reduces the child's need to find out through private (and perhaps unfortunate) experimentation. If talking about how one "does it" is combined with a sensible discussion of when and why, the result should be a workable set of rules for behavior. By way of analogy, it is not enough to give someone a ball and bat and tell the individual to go play baseball. The rules and skills involved must also be understood. Sex information presented out of social, moral and ethical context is *not* a proper substitute for thorough instruction in the range of private and public responsibilities and opportunities that sexual expression involves.

Adult fears that telling boys and girls together about sex is an invitation for them to try it are groundless. Sooner or later, they're going to try it anyway. How much better to preface the attempt with understanding. This is even more important to the brain-handicapped person, who is likely to accept uncritically partial or false information from peers and experience troubling situations in the process.

Teaching contraception is also considered by many

adults to be an inducement to sexual license, the assumption being that if you tell young people how to avoid pregnancy, then the last realistic constraint is eliminated and kids will at once embark upon a binge of promiscuity. Apart from the fact that this attitude does not place much faith in adolescent integrity — and even encourages disrespect *for* integrity — fear of pregnancy has never been much of a constraint, in or out of marriage. Lust, like the oldest profession, exists. Its urgings can only be magnified when expression of the urge is thwarted. If teenagers are regarded as more vulnerable to lust than adults (a dubious proposition in any case), then they are more entitled to know, lacking adult experience, how *not* to bring a child into the world too early for its best care. In short, adult society *knows* that nonprocreative sex is widely practiced and has to stop pretending that it isn't.

The developmentally disabled need to understand these basics, too, but such seemingly difficult concepts are often held to be unteachable. Studies clearly indicate that they are not. As Professor Warren R. Johnson of the University of Maryland has concluded in his contribution to the symposium *Human Sexuality and the Mentally Retarded*, "Contraception education is as feasible for the retarded as other educational undertakings of importance to them."

Among the contraceptive methods available are: the IUD, condom, diaphragm, pill, vasectomy, tubal ligation, vaginal jellies and foams such as Emko. Before advising a young adult, however, or recommending a particular method, it is best for parents to seek professional counsel on what would be most individually appropriate, as well as reading *Contraceptive Technology*, which offers complete and concise information on the subject.

Like a vasectomy or tubal ligation, the IUD does not require a lot of explanation, though anything done to one's body is better done with an explanation than without, and each person should have the right to understand and elect options, if possible. In some instances, parents have had their retarded daughter's tubes tied off after her first period, or a vasectomy performed on a son at maturity, with no attempt to offer reasons why (along with workable alternates), mainly because sex education was to that point omitted. What good does it do to render someone "safe" if the benign uses of sex have only been repressed?

The condom, pill, jellies and foams take instruction: how to use them, when to use them, why to use them. Such instruction may seem awkward when sex information has been previously withheld. But when questions have been answered fairly over the years, talk about contraception follows in a more simplified manner.

Personal hygiene must be taught at the earliest possible age, not with the appearance of the first pubic hair or menstrual flow. Whether or not boys are circumcised, they need to be advised on proper washing of the entire crotch area, changing underpants regularly and recognizing infections. Body odor is, of course, increasingly noticeable during adolescence and can be a source of shame to the child who has not been adequately instructed. For a developmentally disabled young man, any uncleanness is a pronounced social liability as he attempts to make his way in the world.

Hygiene for girls involves all of the foregoing, as well as help in learning to use pads or tampons during menstruation and recognizing the signs of an unhealthy vaginal discharge. Any mother can assist her daughter in developing a sound routine of personal hygiene. But again, preparation must begin early if menstruation, body odor and grooming are to be effectively managed. Itching, both anal and genital, is a common problem for all of us. Most scratch in private, but when a brain-handicapped person has the simple honesty to scratch in public, it is viewed as another sign of unacceptability. Applying a salve isn't enough. If a bacterial or fungal cause exists, it has to be eliminated; and of course, regular bathing habits along with general cleanliness help avoid such possible infections.

The entire objective of attracting and being attracted comes down to achieving positive relationships with family and loved ones. Society upholds this as the ideal, abused though it may be, yet tends to believe that the ideal cannot be reached by the developmentally disabled. Findings indicate otherwise. As Janet Mattinson of the London Institute of Marital Studies has reported, also in *Human Sexuality and the Mentally Retarded*, brain-handicapped couples can often reinforce each other's strengths, actively and effectively. The right to *try*, if one is capable of trying, is a fundamental right of life, as is the truth, from the very beginning, about one's sexuality.

Perhaps the fears of society about sex and the developmentally disabled are based on eugenics and the notion, first suggested by Mendel's laws, that all brain handicap is a matter of "bad genes," that if you put retarded men and women together, they will outbreed everyone else and fill the world with defective children. But we already know that inheritance is not the usual cause of brain handicap. It isn't enough to say that developmentally disabled couples have fewer children than others; we must remember that the vast majority are the children of those who have had no family history of mental disorder. They have been wounded by life. Are we to punish or deny the wounded? Or are we to help?

The fallacy of the eugenic approach is that it is founded upon fear and perpetuates prejudice. It is too often focused on differences held to be threatening, and on the assumption that the threat must be eliminated or restrained — by inhumane measures, if necessary. What this thinking has overlooked is its own illogic, a condition more dire than the dyslogic syndrome it deems a brain defect: if a perceived difference is threatening and completely removed, then what? Each of us is different, so what is the next difference to be wiped out?

In the name of genetic purification, even well-meaning people have argued that we should remove or sterilize anyone with an imperfect gene. If we did this, no one would be around to enjoy the results, including the proponents of this course. For *every* human being carries some genetic weakness. Thomas Jefferson's younger sister, Elizabeth, was severely retarded, James Madison had epilepsy (which was why he married Dolley at forty-three), and John Kennedy had a brain-damaged sister. Is there anyone who breathes who is perfect? Let the claimant stand forth. The individual needs immediate assistance.

Life evolves through differences, not similarities. Our prophets are born and arise from unexpected sources. Even Moses had a speech impediment. It is in our extraordinary genetic flexibility and variety that the future of mankind lies, as it always has, and those who are preoccupied with perfection do not begin to know the meaning, reality and value of compassion that permits the evolutionary process to occur. This is not to disagree with the validity of Darwin's theory of the "survival of the fittest," for clearly the fit of any species are endowed with a better chance to survive. Rather, it is to reassert the call for greater understanding, since man, unlike lower animals, is the only species to be prejudiced against its own kind.

"I give unto ye," Christ said, "a new commandment: that ye love one another" — accept, not fear, excommunicate, purge or crucify.

In accepting the developmentally disabled, we not only help those in need of compassion, we learn to accept each other. In accepting the sexuality of the developmentally disabled, we not only help the brain-handicapped, we learn to accept as both right and good our own sexual expression.

▣ Therapy

WITH MATURATION, A CRITICAL TRANSITION IS reached for both young adult and parents. The child has grown up; the parents have grown older. The child seeks to understand the ways of independence; the parents confront a decline in life. After all the years of daily care, a natural separation approaches, fraught with potential trauma.

In primitive societies when you passed from one stage of life to another, a *rite de passage* allowed you the occasion to be formally initiated into the mysteries of a new phase of existence. But in modern society, vestiges of the *rite de passage*, like graduation ceremonies, tend to be shorn of personal meaning, and people are left to grapple alone in the crowd with deep but inevitable emotional uncertainties. Some parents resist letting go; others may separate, seeking to be young again by changing partners. And the teenager, thrusting out, may experience an identity crisis, accompanied by what Socrates called 2300 years ago "unruly" behavior — the perplexing awareness that childhood is no more and the role of independence not yet clear.

For families with a developmentally disabled youngster, the change is complicated by the fact that the maturing child has fewer opportunities for successful adaptation — as well as by parental habits that are deeply ingrained. It becomes too easy to think that someone with a brain handicap cannot manage independently, and the handicapped offspring has in turn had plenty of persuasion to believe it. Perpetual childhood is not healthy for anyone. Parents become frustrated by continuing overdependence, and the new adult chafes at limitations. As this difficult situation develops in high school, special education tapers off, forcing the parents to assume a greater burden when their load should be reduced. Some handicapped teenagers may already have dropped out, others placed in private programs, and the few remaining grouped in one slow-learner class.

Alas, too, the perpetual-child syndrome only postpones parental confrontation with the inevitable: what happens when they die or become physically unable to manage? For those who have worked creatively over the years, such pangs may be reduced. Even so, close attention must be paid to this period of transition. If parents do not expect too much from school, they will be better prepared for the time when it is over. Home teaching, as distinguished from formal education, has many advantages and should be part of the daily round, regardless of school attendance. But in making best use of the methods, it helps to have some grasp of memory and brain function.

Although often mistakenly thought of as conscious recall, the process of total memory is synonymous with life itself. Partial or cortical memory involves less than ten percent of the brain — the thin surface whose inter-connections are associated with IQ. A computer with the capacity of the total brain, however, might fill a large office building and use enough electricity to power a small city. Final exams test how much you remember of what you have been taught but have little bearing on how you use what you've been taught or how long you will retain it after the exam is over. Academic learning, or the separation of information into subjects with a system of instruction for each, is a different process than funda-mental learning required in the survival association of information, or what is learned in one situation and modified by another. When academic programs become too intense, the student is under enormous pressure not to think but to acquire a mass of data unquestioningly. *Summa cum laude* Super Joe thus may often have a lot of "wising up" to do in trying to apply such data to his daily life.

We all generalize from the particular, as happens when we see someone from a different country and ex-tend individual characteristics to typify national ones. The more difficult task is to particularize from the gen-eral and know when the generalization is inapplicable. Perceiving the exception to the rule forms the basis for the discovery and evolution of new thought. Yet we con-tinue to emphasize conformity and memorization of existing knowledge alone, which restricts our greater mental functions.

Memory — real memory — is something else entirely, and in its vastness as elemental as $E = MC^2$. Chromo-somes, for instance, constitute our Eternal Cells, chemically coded to recall and reproduce the entire structure of life. ("One DNA molecule," observes Leslie A. Hart in *How the Brain Works*, "can hold enough information that in printed form would fill a good-sized library.") This is not done consciously. It is done biochemically in a natural and therefore most rational way. The presence of a Y chromosome clues the mother's system to alter hormonal balance to the fetus in a way that produces a boy instead of a girl. This chemical transfer is similar to cortical reception, coding and relay of information. Experience is stored not just for the sake of storing it but for reproduction, the same way that every single living cell must not only remember how and when to reproduce itself but *do* it. If that memory process is disturbed, the cell either dies, mutates or grows wild. If it happens in the brain, the increasing evidence suggests that symptoms of brain handicap may appear. Indeed, the December 1976 issue of *Yale Alumni Magazine* reported that researchers at Yale University are discovering — as they are at many other centers — that a wide range of mental disorders derive from biochemical errors or deficits.

We seem to be overly impressed by feats of recall, in which the cortex is trained to recite a set of words. Like watching an acrobat, these acts may be entertaining. They are insignificant compared to the feat of recall when sperm and ovum meet and re-create the entire body, billions and billions of cells accurate to the very last submicroscopic detail.

Cortical recitation is also unimpressive when compared with the constant subconscious chatter that goes on between the brain and liver as it monitors nutrients in the blood stream and calculates the exact amount needed from each gland. Failure to detect a minor variation in the systemic pH level alone can cause death. If control of the pituitary at the base of the brain isn't precisely right, body growth is altered. Arriving at puberty, cycling of ovulation, and regulating the term of pregnancy are other intricate codifications. In leukemia, white blood cells biochemically forget their mission; in allergies, sensitized membranes react to nonhazardous substances; and underlying the mystery of crib deaths may be memory loss or interruption in the involuntary centers for breathing. Still, we keep on stressing the cortex to the exclusion — even detriment — of total memory.

Other memory functions involve maintenance of correct body temperature and the endogenous and circadian rhythms, or "body clock," which, in its geophysical relation, is upset by the phenomenon of jet lag, as well as the change from standard to daylight saving time. In sleep, only part of the brain is shut down by the reticular activating system (RAS). The rest actively keeps the body alive at a lower rate to eliminate wastes and ready tissues for reuse. Sleep following illness may be prolonged not because it is prescribed but because it is recalled by the RAS as needed. Memory failure in the RAS may cause insomnia and the other extreme of narcolepsy, or frequent, uncontrollable falling asleep.

When Freud postulated his theory of the subconscious, it was considered revolutionary because concepts of memory were up to that time held to be cortical only, despite the fact that no one could figure out where in the cortex memory was located. Yet even Freud overlooked evidence that memory was far more than could be explained by a theory of layering, or why we can perform multiple tasks simultaneously, such as conscious and unconscious computation, carrying on a conversation and stirring the soup while our thoughts are elsewhere, driving through traffic with great accuracy while projecting answers to unresolved situations, concurrently fantasizing others, the sudden emergence from seemingly nowhere of a bright idea or inspiration.

Following experimental, surgical or accidental brain damage, it has been repeatedly observed, and documented by Karl S. Lashley, that memory loss was in proportion to cell loss; and Kurt Goldstein noted in studies of brain-injured combat veterans that remaining tissue could learn to compensate, that one neuron could substitute for another, in much the same way that other senses become sharper after blindness. Additionally, little attention was paid to the modification of memory caused by stress — physical, environmental, emotional or nutritional.

Nor were the phenomena of instincts, imprinting and extrasensory perception thought to have anything to do with memory. In instincts, such as hibernation, bird migration, the homing of salmon, bees and pigeons, the process was crossed off as unlearned and therefore not remembered. It was not thought that things could be remembered without conscious learning, even though James V. McConnell's well-known flatworm experiments suggested that they were. In these experiments, a flatworm was taught a simple performance. When it was cut up and fed to untaught flatworms, they acquired memory of the performance. Hibernation and migration, too, were indeed learned somewhere and passed on, in the basic survival memory of the organism.

Imprinting, on the other hand, occurs (among other ways) when an animal has been separated from its parents at or soon after birth and is raised by people. Every dog lover has undoubtedly noticed that dogs tend to take on attributes of their owners. But even geese so raised, as I experienced in my boyhood days, will form a V behind their human parent, honking at and attacking intruders. Geese have only a small, primitive central nervous system, but from one day to the next, they remember who is their human parent and who isn't.

Concepts of total memory also lend some credence to a few aspects of astrology. To the extent that early experiences are formative, certain conditions prevailing at birth are primal, though we may have no conscious remembrance of them. If we agree that brain waves are electrical and that electricity is subject to magnetic modification, then geomagnetism, as modified by solar, lunar and planetary influences, may have a bearing on the formation of dendrites and synapses, which are the early bases of thought patterns. Unlearned belief in soul, as well as unlearned superstitions, suggests that we are capable of transmitting to others more mental processes than we give ourselves credit for or are even aware of.

Carl Jung held that since myths and dreams are much the same the world over, people are connected by a "collective unconscious." Putting that another way, the human brain is as evolutionary as the human body and is a history of what has gone on before. Growth of the fetus passes through every step of evolution, similar to that of all lower animals. If the body has vestiges (such as a small tail and second-stomach appendix) of ancient developments, so does the brain have constructs of things long passed. People in "primitive" societies deeply believe in magic, and children in modern society go through this fantasy stage of development. The eventually mature then come to see the natural relation between cause and effect. Since one is no longer mystified by what can be explained, science took on the form of a new religion, almost to the point of asserting that it could replace love rather than contribute to it. The oldest part of the brain is our center for the sense of smell, and we are now coming to understand that it is capable of detecting both conscious and subconscious odors. Conscious odors are strong smells, such as onions. Subconscious odors are trace elements emitted by each living thing. Emotions change what is secreted, and the human sense of that change is what we sometimes call "picking up good or bad vibes."

To limit memory to the cortex and simplistic layering is not unlike postulating that the world is flat and limiting navigation to the known through fear of falling off an edge into the unknown. What man is formally taught is only a minuscule part of his memory capacity. How many words, in how many different languages and dialects, can be created from twenty-six letters? and how many thoughts from the words created? If that is the potential of a handful of symbols, what is the potential of the trillions of dendrites in the brain? As we begin to understand this, the door opens on ways in which we can stimulate use of the total brain, not just aspects of academic learning, which for the developmentally disabled young adult are already confusing.

It is popular to call the management of these elements "therapy." Curious. We don't seem to have exercise anymore. We have physical therapy. Therapists abound in all fields, from speech to massage, doing outstanding and needed work. Yet the clinical connotation of certain forms of therapy is that life can't be merely enjoyable, it should be professionally structured to "do" something for you. Along with the doing, I am sure that each of us welcomes the reward of enjoying, without necessarily having any other purpose *but* enjoyment. Joys are few enough for the brain-handicapped and their parents. So if possible, we ought to avoid excessive reliance on programming stimulation and should increase the potential of plain fun.

Art is one of the most vital forms of communication, using hand and eye to express concrete or abstract images and their interpretation without use of words. Man's ancestors held their cave drawings to be magic, including the symbols that eventually gave rise to alphabets, capable of capturing the essence of life. Our unlearned tribal memory of that ancient magic still persists today in the aura we ascribe to those who create motion pictures on the walls of caves called theaters, or to those who use the alphabet to fix thought on the pages of a publication. This primal sense can be used most effectively in working around a brain disability and helping the person exercise uninjured sections of the mind.

There are three selectives: tool, surface and subject. Each should suit the ability and interests of the artist. If a paintbrush is unmanageable, the tool can be a set of broad-tipped colored felt pens with washable ink or finger paints or crayons. The advantage of felt pens is that they are easy to hold and use, and the colors go on directly, without having to be dipped in liquid pigments. Also, preparation and cleanup are quick, and control of line is simplified. Whatever is selected, it should be within the means of the individual's manual dexterity, not based on parental expectations or preferences.

The same applies to choice of surface — sketch pad, newsprint, cardboard, canvas. A sketch pad of heavy paper is a good surface, adaptable to various tools. It can be placed on the lap, table or floor, and the paper is stiff enough to hang up for display — the reward of artistic endeavor. The right size of surface is also important. Something too large may be difficult to fill, with the image getting crammed into a corner. Too small, and the picture runs off the page. But with experimentation, what works best can be determined.

Additional experimentation is needed in deciding upon subject. Brain handicap often involves problems of perception and conception that make it frustrating to draw a concrete object, such as a box or house. The lines go off in unsatisfactory directions, and there's no point forcing the effort. Instead, expression of an abstract should be encouraged — drawing a memory, dream, feeling, idea; conveying friendship, celebrations, the seasons. When for any reason one subject is not working, the need is to suggest another, until what can be done coincides with the fascination of doing it. Through art and the coordination of hand and eye to reproduce something of personal interest that is attractive to others, unspoken emotions are relieved, often accompanied by improved attention span, verbal abilities and behavior.

Like art, music is a form of communication that stimulates the brain. Sometimes the young adult has the skills to play an instrument and learn to make sounds either by reading music or by imitating. The piano requires coordination of fingers; wind instruments, from clarinet to trumpet, use mouth and hands; and then there are the strings, such as a guitar or violin, that have to be supported while both hands are in operation. If the correct ability is there, the possibility exists of teaching the appropriate instrument. If it isn't, any attempt to force instruction will fall flat and lead to needless disaffection for music expression and appreciation. Better by far to consider the other avenues for experiencing music — radio, television, phonograph. Radio and phonograph offer advantages, particularly when used with a set of headphones that lock in music and shut out background noises. Also, headphones allow the speakers to be turned off should others in the room prefer to talk or read.

What is listened to is perhaps more consequential than *how* it is heard, the smile of appreciation — not formal music appreciation — being the objective. Some parents can't stand classical music, others can't stand pop or modern. Their preferences must not preclude discovery of what most delights their child, who needs to experience pleasure and relaxation through music, enjoy feelings expressed by song. But in addition to using instruments and recordings, singing together as a family can be wonderfully pleasurable — something we tend to forget today amidst the many inducements of passive entertainment. When the family sings together for fun, no matter who can or cannot carry a tune, they initiate another form of unlearned memory: the tribe convened to sing night into day, banish darkness both within and without, bring rains and good hunting, share feelings with one another beyond the reach of words. Community sings, as well as sing-along shows, hymns at places of worship or songs at school, fulfill much the same role. When helped to join in such opportunities to the extent feasible, the brain-handicapped person finds a way of belonging, of being part of what others are doing for mutual enjoyment.

Our center of speech hearing is located in a different part of the brain than our center for music hearing. With a developmental disability, the use of words can be an unclear, arduous task. Do we mean what we say, or say what we mean? This is complex enough for any of us. It may become profoundly frustrating for someone who has a speech impediment, limited vocabulary or word inversion. When PhDs struggle to get a thought over in a paragraph of three-syllable words, what of someone who has to communicate in a three-word sentence of broken, monosyllabic sounds? It doesn't mean that the person's need isn't both real and intelligent; it means that this individual is having a hard time choosing and using sounds to form expression understandable to others. Fourteen and a half million Americans have speech or hearing problems. The assumption that someone doesn't know what is being said just because of a speech impediment is a dangerous one. Even dogs know words without being able to say them. (And since cats use body language, with notable use of tail, perhaps a tailless Manx can be said to have a speech impediment.) Yet the inability is often interpreted as a sign of stupidity and made fun of, which further inhibits the handicapped person's will to try. After puberty, speech difficulties reduce social acceptability — ironic, as well as unfortunate, when you consider that we otherwise laud the "man of few words."

A speech problem can be helped, both at home and at school, if it is approached not in the spirit of correcting but of inviting. In some instances, certain sounds — vowels or consonants — are hard to pronounce. In others, they are out of sequence, *celery* becoming *ler-cer-ry.* Youngsters with a brain handicap are already so corrected and criticized they may resist any reminder that their use of words is incorrect. But by inviting someone who says *lercery* to eat a piece of *celery*, with mouth movements being exaggerated enough for imitation, instruction becomes a reality, not an embarrassment — a desire to please, not a command against displeasing. For speech, tongue, throat and lips have to coordinate to form an understandable word. Incorrect patterns are usually learned through indifference or neglect. Relearning a correct pattern takes place by trying to imitate someone who patiently cares and who is admired, with the triumph of success being as elating as any triumph.

In dancing, the body responds to rhythm for reasons of pleasure, not the fulfillment of a productive task. It is also a form of physical language. With puberty, of course, dancing additionally takes on social connotations, couples attracting each other or gaining group approval through performance. To some degree, however, we appear to have construed the art as a matter of standing up and jigging around — impossible or undesirable in some forms of cerebral palsy, awkward for those of us who seem endowed with two left feet. But in the real sense, dancing is the pleasurable use of any part of the body in relation to sound and the movement of someone else, and it once again employs unlearned tribal memories of ceremonial, festive or ritual occasions. As nonverbal communication, dancing is a way of conveying — and gaining approval for — a variety of feelings that are spontaneous, responsive and imitative. This makes it a form of dramatic play, stimulating brain use and expanding mental abilities, as well as improving body condition.

Manual training, sports, exercise, work and hobbies are other activities of great value to the teenager in building confidence in physical performance. Regular hours should be blocked out for work, exercise and sports. Apart from helping with household chores, every adolescent benefits from doing paid work. In most neighborhoods there are various odd jobs — washing, cleaning, sweeping, raking, weeding, painting, delivering newspapers. Parental encouragement and assistance help open opportunities, and the young worker learns the responsibilities of holding a job, the pride of receiving pay for service rendered. As for reasonable exercise, a few minutes every morning of activating the limbs stimulates circulation and tones the body for work and sports.

In high school athletics, brain-handicapped students are usually sidelined on one pretext or another. Perhaps this comes from the view that sports are meant for *winning*: that when a person merely wishes to participate, it is not enough. Of course, schools do have intramural sports and physical education, as well as varsity and junior varsity teams, but the majority of students, with or without a developmental disability, still seem to wind up as spectators instead of being included in competition and encouraged to enjoy making best use of their physical attributes. Many young handicapped men and women can swim, bowl or play ball very well. Their health, and that of others, could be aided through a broader, more comprehensive educational attitude toward sports, for growing is playing, and playing is fundamental to life.

If school athletics are out, for whatever reason, and there are no after-school vacant-lot athletics, activity centers have sports programs and intercenter meets that lead up to a "Special Olympics" for the developmentally disabled. Just as important as endeavoring to join in these is the effort to establish family sports, which should be a set part of every week — bowling or swimming, skating, pitch-and-catch, backyard basketball, even shooting pool. For sporting goes back in brain evolution beyond the beginnings of man to the colt and stallion at play. It doesn't make any difference who's "best." Each of us has an individual best. Trying to reach it is the basis of sports therapy.

Manual training and hobbies fill a wide variety of interests through body use, too. Manual training does not necessarily mean using power tools, which require minimal exertion and need to be thoroughly safeguarded. Rather, it is a matter of training manual skills to create some desirable object — basket, sweater, belt, bookends, pot, whatever. Clay is an especially good medium. Items attractive around home can also be sold, and the making of them is a tangible, three-dimensional art that uses imagination as it improves dexterity. Interesting rocks can be collected and decorated for paperweights, epoxied to make little animals, or polished in a rock grinder to create jewelry; discarded bones can be sun-bleached, colored and glued together to form lamp stands or other items. In some cases, manual training may *be* the hobby, though hobbies range from stamp-collecting to model-building — fascinations that, shared or private, brighten a rainy day, as they did when our ancestors made pots and arrowheads in caves.

For the brain-handicapped, the essentials of breathing and posture, grooming and appearance, are sometimes neglected on the mistaken assumption that any deficit in these areas must be an associated symptom. However, dress and manners are learned. Anyone is going to slouch and become sloppy in the face of prolonged rejection. A developmentally disabled youngster faces rejection every day and tends to adopt the ways that confirm unacceptability. Early lessons in correct posture improve mental attitude, promote good breathing and healthy physical growth. Parents cannot force good posture, but they can teach and encourage it, as they help their child learn how to groom neatly and dress attractively. Presentability increases self-confidence and self-esteem. To be greeted with a smile makes the whole day smile.

Another common difficulty is expressing anger. It is frustrating for any of us to cope in a difficult world. It is even more frustrating to cope in the face of impossible expectations. Yet someone with a brain handicap is often required to have no anger at all. Super Joe can strike back because he was punched, and Mother and Dad can speak crossly because they've had a rough day; but if a boy with epilepsy strikes a tormentor, he is apt to be looked upon as a threat; or if a retarded girl cries because she has been teased, the tendency is to consider her emotionally unstable. There are so many unreasonable limitations placed on these children, demanding the individual to be anger-free in every type of situation, to bottle up emotion until it either becomes unbearable or is sublimated into other behaviors — like having "an accident," secretly breaking something, perhaps persecuting a small animal.

There are many effective ways of expressing anger that keep it from being displaced on someone or something not involved, or letting it turn inward. Anger turned inward is anger dangerous to all. Anger displaced simply provokes more anger. We may not be able to answer back at the boss because he has been hostile in the office instead of letting his wife know that he can't stand her extravagances; and by the same token, students may not be entitled to challenge the teacher who scolds the class instead of responding to the criticism of a spouse. But we certainly can vent anger without abusing bystanders if we admit that it exists and that the healthy response is to express it simply and directly by initiating an appropriate activity or inquiry.

For many people, anger is sometimes diverted into fascination with collision sports, in cries of "kill the umpire," in going to movies to see the good guys win over the bad guys. The brain-handicapped teenager may not have or be able to make best use of these outlets but can be encouraged, at least, to draw a picture of anger, perhaps talk it out with a sympathetic listener or work a punching bag — whatever form of release that harms no one while defusing the destructive impulse.

The true act of turning the other cheek is an excellent way of walking tall in the face of petty meanness, and to be able to forgive is a sign of internal strength that frees the mind from dwelling on bygone hard moments. When dependence upon home creates frustrations for the developmentally disabled teenager — as it does for practically any teenager — parents can help relieve the situation by arranging for "overnights" elsewhere, with friends or relatives. Such frustrations may show up in withdrawn, erratic or petulant behavior. Even if they don't, time away from family is good for *both* parents and youngster, allowing them to return to routine with renewed enthusiasm.

In many regions, there are fine summer camps for the brain-handicapped, after the child is old enough to feel secure at such places. Camping is good for the growth and development of most children. A developmentally disabled person especially needs social interaction independent of parents and school, and the outdoors is a splendid area for self-discovery. Local agencies and activity centers have lists of recommended summer camps. Where none is available, parents should look to car-camping or backpacking.

Backpacking requires sturdy legs, so car-camping is indicated when there is a problem of physical mobility. It can be done with purchased equipment but is just as well done with homemade gear, if everyone in the family is drawn into planning and making things unhurriedly throughout the school year — stitching rip-stop nylon for a tarp tent, preparing blanket rolls, checking publications for tips, figuring out together where to go, what to do and what is needed to do it. Though done away from home in the open air car-camping has become a highly social experience, and many public campgrounds run by state or federal governments now offer group programs — nature walks, campfire sings — in which one family joins with others, both young and old.

Backpacking has a different set of advantages, including interdependence in the wilderness, and the planning for it involves the family as a whole, whether gear is purchased or made, for the full academic year: united action toward a long-range goal to avoid the errors of haste. Those who have never backpacked should carefully study camping literature, equipment catalogues, maps and the like, draw up lists of food and gear, and make the first treks short, along well-marked trails, or join up with a family experienced in backpacking.

Whatever the form of camping — by car, backpacking, boat or bicycle — the familiar four walls are left behind for awhile. In their absence, sensory experience is varied and the family gains new perspectives, activating ancient urges that trace to the time when early man knew the freedom, discipline and responsibility of being part of nature.

Perhaps the most serious problem for a brain-handicapped teenager is lack of friends. Personality is not improved by social isolation, yet isolation is what such young men and women face regularly. The label acquired early is passed on through school, and it rarely says what the individual does well, mostly points to presumed weaknesses associated with the disability, which makes others stay away. Without being able to learn from them, the person may learn alone to relate things in a disorganized manner and have greater difficulty controlling impulses. Not infrequently, impulsive delinquency may result.

In any remedial program, we must try to bear in mind that up to this point the developmentally disabled young adult has had less of everything, and so we are dealing in every sense with forms of deprivation — social, emotional, educational, as well as physical and mental. By treating the symptoms instead of trying to fix blame, we can do a great deal to assist. When lack of appeal is the continuing problem, it can often be corrected by programs in behavior training. When social immaturity persists, punishment isn't the answer. Professional counseling is required to reduce parental overprotection and to overcome emotional deficits. When feelings of inferiority are evident, achievement demands that create frustration and fear have to be minimized, usually through out-of-home placement. And when there are difficulties of impulse control, the need is to check for potential bad influences and reduce loneliness by enrollment in an adult activity center.

Those who have struggled through the bewilderment of education under deprived circumstances either quit or emerge with confused work habits, inability to make decisions, poor writing skills. The waiting world offers such persons counterculture pressures, few jobs, no dates, driving restrictions and limited places to stay. Nonetheless, they are supposed to know how to manage a budget, keep house and do other things required for independent living. Their primary urge may be to seek a return to security, cling to the few who cared, not understanding that separation has to come about. And what, if anything, has been accomplished by the years of in-school instruction?

Social, emotional, educational *and* vocational training must be integrated parts of the whole. Academics have value, but the best of academics doesn't signify much if the student has little understanding of how to get along with others, respect self and earn a living. If frank and complete sex education is as important as learning to read, then practical instruction on dress, behavior, decision-making, housekeeping, work habits and skills is at least as important as learning to count.

Therapy is supposed to be curative. All the therapy in the world doesn't amount to much when a person's only opportunity on leaving school is not a place in industry but a place — despite abilities — on welfare rolls in a sheltered workshop. Some industries have, at long last, agreed to hire the developmentally disabled, *if* they have learned a job skill and how to cope. Such progress appears to have its advantages, too: as reported by the September 1976 *Memo* from California's Area I Developmental Disabilities Board, DuPont rated handicapped workers ninety-one percent average or better in production and ninety-six percent average or better in safety compared with nonhandicapped workers.

Let us hope that, in time, more doors will open; for there is no greater therapy on earth than the dignity of belonging through earning a living.

▣ Nutrition and the Environment

NUTRITION AND THE ENVIRONMENT INTERACT WITH each other and are intimately related to the well-being of mankind. Both can account for changes in behavior, intelligence, physical stamina and emotional stability. The way we live conditions what and how we eat; what and how we eat alters the way in which we live. Since critical impoverishment of one or the other can lower physical resistance to infection and disease, as well as slow recovery from both, it is imperative that we endeavor to attack the sources of such stress as an integral part of the treatment of illnesses and our overall concepts of child development. Yet nutritional education remains a largely neglected area in medicine. Much the same applies to education in environmental medicine. Of the $125 billion spent annually on health care, very little of it goes to either.

Today, the environment is popularly equated with conservation: preserving the wilderness, keeping air and water from being irreparably polluted. Clean air and water, uncontaminated food, and maintaining the balance of nature essential to life on earth are obviously of key importance, but environment in the broader sense is defined by the dictionary as *all* external conditions and influences affecting life, development, human behavior and society. For families with a brain-handicapped child, the immediate aspects that can be individually improved or worsened are housing, family life, neighborhood and occupation.

Someone living under residential duress is not apt to feel especially keen about saving a tree, cleaning up for others, or supporting air and water quality programs. Relief becomes the focal desire — any relief, no matter how small or temporary. But when there's something worth living for, respect for life around expands. Pain of any sort is, by definition, traumatic, and bad housing is a chronic emotional trauma that may retard a child's ability to learn, evolve and adapt, just as it can undermine adult perception and motivation. Bad housing does not necessarily relate to poverty circumstances or, in the other extreme, palatial isolation. After all, Eskimos have gotten along in igloos and royalty has enjoyed its castles. Rather, it tends to involve structures in which there is little sense of personalized place, in and out of doors, with inadequate variety or reduced opportunity for relief from others. Perhaps no housing is ever "best" and all housing "good" if it houses a stable family. However, when instabilities do appear, it is inappropriate to ascribe them to some familial "fault" without having a look at the potentially negative influences of the physical home environment. If the structure is for some reason wearing upon everyone living in it, the rewards of life are diminished for them, and that feeling of deprivation conditions what they do elsewhere.

Interpersonal stresses within the family, not related to housing, can be equally problematical. Common sources are: divided authority, death or divorce, domestic discord and prolonged illness. Divided authority sometimes occurs when a third adult lives with the family or is visiting indefinitely. Without meaning to, that person may take over or modify decisions that should be the parents', intruding upon the way they discipline the youngsters, perhaps making it awkward for them to air their disagreements. As children begin to perceive duality in established authority and learn to utilize it, further tension is created. Similarly, battles, breakups and the death or disability of a family member can alter the emotional well-being of all and influence their performance away from home, in a manner difficult for each to handle and especially so for the brain-handicapped.

Stress from the neighborhood is evidenced in two ways: ethnic or socioeconomic prejudice, and the demands of overconformity. In an atmosphere of community hostility, it is unreasonable to expect parents and children not to be in some way negatively touched by it. And in the case of overconformity, where all is too much alike, there is tremendous pressure not to stray from perceived standards and to regard anyone who does as a potential threat. Both environments are to a certain extent conditioned by fear, which tends to make people behave defensively, limits options in friendships and social activities, and shapes what family members think are the "acceptable" ways of getting along together.

Occupational stress stems from what one is doing and where it is being done, whether at school or at work. It is a laudable drive to achieve, to gain success, to "make it." But if the occupation has shrinking rewards, one's motivation for work is reduced, although the work still has to be done in order to avoid loss of standing, social or financial. How painful the constant, perhaps unexpressed sense of having to drag oneself through the day. If these feelings are sufficiently intense and unrelieved, they can alter behavior, sometimes provoking unrelated angers within the home, and the individual with a chronic disability may, in such situations, come to be seen as a chronic irritant.

Programs for the treatment of brain handicap are in jeopardy if surrounding circumstances for the family incline to be emotionally crippling. Sometimes people don't recognize such stresses because they have become so used to them. Sometimes they are seen and ignored in the hope that they will go away, or in the belief that nothing can be done. Doctors, social workers and others who are concerned often find their best efforts stymied when afflicted families become too vulnerable to a negative environment, of whatever sort, and manifest an inability to rectify it. So much *can* be done by facing the problem head-on and looking for acceptable options. Indeed, no one is really trapped unless passively resigned to believe in the trap.

Locating a place where the brain-handicapped can get around without undue hazard, in the city, suburb or country, follows an understanding of the primary aspects of a counterproductive environment and recognition that they have to be changed. Bad situations usually grow from taking too much for granted — school, neighborhood, residence, water and air, noise, occupation — on the basis of assumed convenience or presumed necessity. Parents with a developmentally disabled youngster are sometimes more prone than others to make hurried decisions because they feel distracted and want to move in quickly in order to get on with things. Then come the unhappy discoveries and all that is attendant upon them.

By carefully reviewing the total environment, using a checklist and rating alternatives, many families can improve their circumstances, perhaps saving money into the bargain. It helps to spend a few hours a weekend for several months looking options over, first on an area basis, then narrowing down to a few communities in it. Is the teaching staff at school appreciated by students? Is the house or apartment cheerful, with adequate privacy and minimal noise pollution? How clean are air and water? Are the streets reasonably free of unsafe traffic? What are the services and tax rate? Where are shopping centers located and are they congenial? Much can often be determined about a community by purchasing something at the nearest grocery store, noting what it offers and asking the clerk a few questions. A poorly managed store may reflect neighborhood indifference, and an irritable clerk can be the product of local frustrations. Finding one place that appeals to every member of the family means comparing notes and talking things over together — as well as observing carefully the performance of the brain-handicapped child. Can the youngster get about with ease and enjoy useful activities? What are the recreational resources? How do others respond in social situations?

Foul air is an observable hazard. If trees and car paint are affected by air pollution, so are people. Children living under conditions of excessive smog may have higher accumulations of lead in their tissues than those raised in clean air, and certain heavy metals such as lead are implicated in impaired brain growth. But breathing bad air is more than a health problem contributing to disease, it must also be considered a stress factor. When body and mind have to operate on oxygen inhaled with contaminants, it stands to reason that the system is more apt to be strained by routine and exceptional demands. In our experience, too, we have noted that dream sleep, so necessary to mental health, appears to be either lowered or modified by unclean air, for reasons as yet not investigated by research. (Indeed, some experts believe that the incidence of neuroses prevalent among affluent societies — a phenomenon of increasing concern to psychiatric specialists — may have more to do with environmental factors than with affluence, per se.)

Noise pollution is another constant source of stress. Day and night, the auditory centers of the brain may be bombarded by the cacophony of strident sounds. In some situations, people become so accustomed to shutting it out as background that they do not connect excessive stimulation with frayed nerves, erratic thinking, and emotional confusion from shallow, restless sleep. Their behavior is then unsettling to the handicapped youngster, as is the noise pollution.

Water quality is also vital to physical and mental health. There are many aspects of pure water that differentiate it from "purified water." Unusual acidity and chemicals in solution, over and above what is naturally indigenous to a particular area, are two considerations. Highly acid water may contribute to joint problems and a variety of intestinal complaints. Since acid corrodes copper pipes, the presence of blue staining below sink faucets is an indicator that the supply should be checked for possible neutralizing by feeding it through a tank of dolomite (calcium-magnesium carbonate). Some people with high intestinal acidity experience upset when drinking daily from a slightly acid source; and in reverse, an alkaline supply tends to lower intestinal acidity needed for digestion. All this suggests is that we should not take water for granted and, when in doubt, have it tested both by Public Health and by a plumber specializing in water conditioning systems. The large mail-order companies also offer free testing.

At the very least, the subject of chemical or mineral contamination is complex. Some chemicals may actually be helpful, others harmful, and several a combination of both. For instance, mercury — ingested from any source —damages young and old alike, whereas lithium carbonate has been associated with reducing mood disorders, according to the National Institute for Mental Health; and chlorine, used to kill dangerous bacteria, sometimes cuts down the population of symbiotic intestinal bacteria. Then too, one source of stress from water — especially in farm areas relying on wells — may involve the leaching into water tables of approved agricultural and industrial chemicals, such as the nitrates and nitrites of fertilizers. So in general, it is important to bear in mind that the whole fluid chemistry of body and brain is tied to the quality of what enters the mouth from a glass, and not to overlook it in the event of a chronic physical or mental difficulty.

If we are to some degree what we drink, we are to a similar degree what we eat. According to Dr. Gerald I. Sugarman of New York, hyperactivity is a symptom of brain disability, may be caused by nutritional stress, and affects at least one child in every classroom of every public school, with the actual number probably much higher. Dr. Benjamin F. Feingold of San Francisco has experienced success in alleviating hyperactivity by modifying diets. And Dr. Lendon H. Smith of Oregon reports that children's behavior can be positively modified by injections of vitamins C and B. Serious nutritional deficiencies, either of specific nutrients or of adequate food intake, impair brain function and, as indicated, the undernourished individual is not only more prone to illness but also does not respond as well to treatment when ill.

Environmental stress may radically alter what is eaten and how it is digested. Under tension, the adrenal glands are activated, and less time is apt to be given to preparing food. Most convenience items eaten in pressured circumstances tend to be high in overly refined sugar, too much of which may cause hypoglycemia, clinically identified as low blood sugar. That in turn depletes the adrenal glands, causing nervousness and more stress. For relief, a drug is usually taken to reduce emotional agitation. That pacifies the brain while giving the liver another complexity to handle. We've become a nation of refined sugar-eaters, with even orange juice getting the sweet treatment. Medical literature now abounds with examples of potential hazards — and one senses that we are witnessing only the tip of the iceberg.

Instantized foods use preservatives, artificial flavors and colors (Red Dyes #2 and #40 have been banned by the FDA as cancer-producing) that may contribute to biochemical brain imbalance. More than three thousand additives are in the American diet. The nitrates and nitrites in smoked meats, hot dogs and coldcuts appear to increase sensitivity to allergens and to create headaches, influencing the central nervous system and requiring medication. Heavily processed, these foods then have to have some nutritional values added, but the trace elements, which are part of whole foods, remain absent. The cost of this combination of color, taste, starch and vitamins is substantially higher than the cost of multivitamin pills. Thus the poor often wind up paying more for less and, as Dr. Denis P. Burkitt of Great Britain has postulated, the lack of fibers in such foods may cause disease, or at least impede the system's ability to prevent disease.

Protein synthesis in the brain is required for memory, and many emotional disorders stem from some malfunction of basic metabolism. Dr. Frederick Goodwin, chief of the psychiatric section of the National Institute for Mental Health, indicates that a single brain amine system could be at fault in many psychotic disorders, and this position — of a link between biochemistry and mental illness — is also supported by Dr. Seymour S. Kety of Harvard and many others. Vitamin B_1 in large doses can change mood. Vitamin C detoxifies medication taken to control epilepsy. Megavitamin therapy has been used with apparent success in some cases of schizophrenia. There are also indications that it may help autism. The principal difficulty in replicating orthomolecular treatment by those not trained in it appears to relate to the omission of some components and to the fact that each person must receive a highly individualized program over a substantial period of time.

Serious reduction of blood sugar — often caused by ill-advised diets popular among those who want to lose weight at an unhealthy speed — can lead to unprovoked tears and other outbursts. To restore a sense of stability, some people may resort to excessive use of alcohol. This carbohydrate initially acts as a stimulant, then as a depressant. Alcohol also dehydrates the system. In cases of chronic alcoholism — as opposed to moderate social drinking — the individual suffers from improper nutrition. The drink is taken as a pick-me-up and emotional restorative. Generally, it is consumed without adding water, in order to hasten the desired effect. The need for food, which is the primary demand, is dampened, and as dehydration sets in, more straight alcohol is sought to quench thirst and allay depression. On recovering, the system's call for food and water is even greater, compounded by feelings of guilt and answered again by the bottle. Studies by Dr. Richard Mattson of Yale Medical

School reveal that alcohol increases seizures by eighty-five percent. With alcoholism now disabling millions of people, perhaps it is time that we recognize it as a nutritional brain disorder and included it as a brain handicap.

Whole foods form the basis for developing and preparing a comprehensive, beneficial diet. The five groups are: (1) milk and milk products (cheese, yogurt); (2) protein (meat, fish, poultry); (3) fruits; (4) vegetables; (5) grain and grain products (bread, cereal). These should be eaten in a balanced manner, within recommended levels of caloric intake over three meals. Families who take the time, once a week, to sit down and confer about planning menus and drawing up the shopping list, with attention to specials, not only eat better and avoid overweight but save money — directly at the market, and indirectly through having fewer health problems. As the importance of proper eating habits is understood, the role of preparation gains respect, mealtime becomes a glad occasion, and the work of cleanup is shared, reducing much of the anxiety that may lead to bad eating habits in the first place.

So many good diets exist, based on enjoyable menus, that trying to recommend one ideal diet can be an exercise in futility. Each family has a different set of preferences, and to explore the pleasures of good eating is itself a pleasure.

From an economic standpoint, the prices of specific foods change with seasonal supply and harvesting, and menus should of course be modified depending upon cost and availability. But in general, a whole cereal is better and cheaper than one machined into a visually appealing shape, just as an unpeeled potato is better than one peeled, unpolished rice better than the polished variety. Lean beef has advantages (including lower price) over attractively marbled steak, and natural, unprocessed foods over their more expensive processed counterparts.

The convention of the hot dog and cold cut came into being as a good way of using up meat scraps that couldn't otherwise be sold, and it was an art in the early days. Now their contents, approved by law, are largely milled cornmeal and soybeans, artificially flavored and colored. Until the situation changes, it is cheaper and healthier to use the cornmeal and soybeans directly. Perhaps one way of helping people using food stamps to eat a balanced diet might be to limit stamps to the purchase of whole foods in the five groups, evenly divided, although some authorities believe that this could prove unworkable or unfair.

Special attention should be given to the diet of the brain-handicapped child when visible problems include: underweight, overweight, low stature, bad teeth, trouble chewing or swallowing, loose bowels, frequent vomiting, odd food preferences. The presence of one or more of these symptoms calls for medical *and* nutritional counsel to ensure that the diet not only is balanced but is properly ingested and digested.

What a family eats is critical. Scarcely less critical is the matter of *when* and *how* each family eats. Good food has to be spaced regularly so that blood sugar levels are maintained. Adequate digestion doesn't occur if eating is pressured by haste or conflict. Young children often become fretful just before meals not because they're seeking attention but because the blood sugar has dropped and the young body does not have sufficient reserves to pick it up on an empty stomach. A wholesome premeal snack instead of a whack is the answer. Far from spoiling the appetite, it may enhance it.

Breakfast is the time when most people rush to get going and shouldn't. Forty percent of one's energy comes from an adequate, unhurried breakfast. It also sets the tone for work. Yet too often breakfast becomes the least satisfactory meal of the day. Then follow the midmorning hungers that have to be staved off with some processed sugar item (or, as Winnie-the-Pooh would say at 11:00 A.M., "a little something" — and for a bear with very little brain, he made a pretty shrewd choice in honey, which is probably the most quickly assimilated of all foods). This situation can be corrected by organization: preparing lunches the night before, setting the breakfast table then, determining the menu, assigning chores and the hour of rising. When breakfast is a rewarding experience rather than something to be gotten out of the way, family members tend to look forward to it, cheerfully coming to the table on time. Even in situations where some have to leave for work earlier than others, there is rarely any reason why, with adequate organization, all can't participate instead of eating in shifts.

Lunch nowadays is not usually an occasion for reconvening the family, since the distance to school or work prohibits returning home. Dinner, therefore, is the focal meal of the day. Here, the main difficulty is that everyone can feel tired from work, perhaps disinclined to do the labor of cooking. However, if the menu has been planned and the basics prearranged, the task is simplified by requiring all to pitch in. Someone can fix a predinner tray of carrot and celery sticks, or cups of hot soup, perhaps glasses of milk for the kids. (Wine, beer or a cocktail certainly have a place in the ritual for many parents.) Equally healthy predinner (and also prebed) snacks are granola, parched soybeans and logan bread. If these are made up on weekends, they can last the week through.

Unity, assistance and cooperation are the prelude to the overture of dinner. Some families like to say or sing a prayer of thanks when they sit down and before they eat. Others may hold hands, observe a moment of silence, or simply celebrate with expressions of approval. Whatever the preference, it is the spirit of being together, enjoying each other in serenity, which makes dinner a happy occasion, and that nourishment is as powerful as the fare, prefacing evening and sleep with a sense of being at ease.

◉ Society

MANY ASPECTS OF LIFE SEEM CONDUCIVE TO FEAR: failure, rejection, sexuality, aging — the list is long, the causes real, the feeling natural. But while fear has been with us ever since thunderstorms and saber-toothed tigers drove every man trembling into his cave, two aspects without parallel in history combine to make fear unnaturally destructive to mental health today. One involves a form of depersonalization that often obliges each of us to cope with fear alone, increasing our learned sense of helplessness. The other is the technology of communication that swiftly transmits action pictures of fearful events from distant places. Both are framed by our awareness, sometimes suppressed in disbelief, that we may have perilously upset natural balances: overpopulated the earth, exploited life-support resources, established huge institutions than can turn upon us. With all this, who needs doomsday weaponry?

Experiencing ever-present fear while feeling unable to talk about it, some people go through a separation from reality so profound that to them the news media seem to be lying, or perhaps conspiring to create bad news. Others participate in acts of violence and terrorism, as if the system were some sort of mean parent best punished by internecine hostility. There are even those who resort to witchcraft, black magic and other cults in an effort to restore the lost sense of personal power, or who trip out chemically, perhaps withdraw into insular communities — the "victim" overcompensating as the only alternative to knuckling under. Instead of relieving fear, these various recourses only add to it, making us all begin to feel a bit bewildered and confused and wonder what hope there is for mankind if *un*reason prevails. Moreover, fearful persons tend to idolize their own beliefs and opinions, which inclines them to acrimonious contest with those who hold different ones, precluding the learning process of open discussion. As an extension of this mentally unhealthy climate, fear of mental ill health itself can on the one hand destroy an exemplary career through whispered insinuations, and on the other allow a seriously disturbed individual to assume unwarranted public and private powers.

Deep, unexpressed fears have given rise to industries devoted to selling reassurance. And there is certainly nothing wrong with what helps us feel some modicum of comfort. However, *non*superficial reassurance that endures simply cannot be bought. It has to begin inside oneself, in the spirit of faith, hope and love. We do not need degrees to become human, medals to become important. Nor can we expect affluence to solve all problems. Perhaps symptomatic of our illusions about what reassures is the "Star Trek" cult, in which the outer-space family of tomorrow remains youthful as it staves off hostile forces, rights all wrongs. What of *this* world,

today, where in the name of humanity so many programs for people seem to have rendered people incidental?

Out of fear, we keep devising increasingly fearful
instruments of war. Everyone decries war while selling
and buying arms, but have we really done anything to
reduce the fear that causes it? Proponents of physical
superiority, seemingly afraid to get along in peace, also
tend to be the proponents of war, in which these her-
alded superiors kill each other. How can that be regarded
as contributing in any way to the improvement of society, physically or mentally? It takes courage to step
out of the false security of ever more powerful weapons
and into the defenseless position of peace and goodwill.
But throughout the ages, we have considered doing so
as a weakness, not a strength — a pleasant circumstance
if one can afford such a luxury. A vaster maturity is
needed to see the difference between "fighting to save"
and losing through hatred. And our salvation is not just
the responsibility of one people but of all people. For
winning at any cost can mean defeat; while learning to
rise above the inevitable setbacks of life can lead to
victory.

We must not, of course, under any circumstances permit or condone destructive actions; nor is it rational for
us to expect that threats and threatening situations will
soon disappear. But at least equal to the task of responding to hostilities is the challenge of ameliorating the
circumstances that create them. Compassion, which
eliminates fear, has many facets and expressions. Prejudice born of fear, on the other hand, has been the same

throughout the ages — even to using the same words. Thus if we check Boston newspapers of the 1850s, following the Irish potato famine, we find almost the identical ugly adjectives used to describe the Irish that were later applied to blacks. So, too, spoke the Egyptians about their Hebrew slaves and, thousands of years later, the Israelis about the Arabs . . . and society about the developmentally disabled. As W. C. Fields once remarked, "I am free of prejudice. I hate them all."

Fear, and inhibitions about talking of it, may underlie social reactions to brain handicap and the establishment of programs that tend to replace individual roles and responsibilities. Thus instead of caring directly for people, we seem to have "delivery systems" governed by so many regulations that it becomes difficult to deliver anything. In time, the main expenditure of energy may be given over more to internal debates about procedures than to getting other work done. This is not good for those in need, nor is it good for those in the system whose ideas and creativity are thwarted.

If we haven't begun to define what we mean by normal, or even the value of being normal, how can we possibly devise meaningful programs to "normalize" someone? Have we yet asked ourselves how different is petit mal from daydreaming? fear from paranoia? imagination from hallucination? repetition from autism? trembling from palsy? innocence from retardation? role-playing from schizophrenia? cramps from convulsions? And why is it that we call talking to God, as in prayer, socially acceptable but consider it mentally suspect if a person claims to hear God talking back?

Perhaps unanswered questions about brain disabilities arise in large measure from unanswered questions about ourselves, or questions unasked because of the awareness that the clown is right, that in each of us there may be something a little aberrant. So it becomes more "comfortable" to avoid candid discussion of deeply human issues, on the one hand separating ourselves from those perceived as different, on the other establishing sheltered services intended to "normalize" them. Are the developmentally disabled animal or human? If we say animal, then the SPCA should be helped to defend the defenseless. If we say human, then the denial of any human right is intolerable, beginning with the right to be directly loved and cared for, not programmed.

"Civilization," quipped Mark Twain, "is a limitless multiplication of unnecessary necessities." Undoubtedly the quip could apply to any period in history, though today we seem close to discovering some limits and, for the brain-handicapped, verge on cutting back *necessary* necessities. As purchasing power diminishes through inflation while money demands rise, we all experience the financial pinch that forces us to revise our priorities in an effort to eliminate what we can do without. In public budgets, usually the first thing cut is adequate funding for mental health. The basic needs of the disabled are thus marginally met, in a way that only creates greater expenses later on, placing us in the position of always being behind, instead of in front of, the problems. Since this drift is accompanied by concepts of progress without change, we must wonder what the future holds.

In our effort to understand the brain, we are in a

very much larger sense engaged in the battle to banish ignorance and improve the quality of life. In this, I suspect that the layman's leadership may be signal. Just as bicycle mechanics first flew, so perhaps we shall see public policy for a government of, by and for the people — all people — get off the ground through the efforts and ingenuity of those not constrained by presumed impossibilities.

At times it almost seems as if a new form of beggary were going on. The truly needy must be helped, yet those with little need are often in the best position to obtain assistance. Sheer volume of demand then makes agency paperwork overwhelming, further adding to the problems of screening out unnecessary requests for public funds. When those without need can get handouts from government, those with need tend to suffer. The graver consequences are manifold. Not only does the private sector of our economy become increasingly burdened, limiting the growth of job opportunities, but also it becomes more difficult for individual initiative to flourish. If it is rewarding to be dependent and punishing to be independent, who then shall conceive of the new ways to advance humanitarianism and prevent social demoralization?

Through unfettered talent, a great opportunity exists to use television in dramatic portrayals of real information about brain handicap; for public attitude and awareness about mental disorders are indispensable to bringing about necessary improvements in our courses of action to better the growth of all children. Many laws have been reformed, and concepts are changing with regard to voting and employment, sex and marriage for the developmentally disabled, but it still comes down to the man in the street and our need through enlightenment to correct widespread misconceptions. Ninety-six percent of the population have television sets. While each child spends 12,000 hours in school from grades one through twelve, each child also spends an average of 15,000 hours watching television during those same years. In a society where money largely controls programming, one prays that sponsors will pay more attention to *what* is being viewed along with how many are viewing.

New knowledge is discovered on the basis of intuition, and even scientists pick and choose what facts to relate. Yet the common assumption is that proof must preface knowledge, rather than knowledge leading to changeable proof; that data-gathering is conclusive, when it is but a sampling of existing probabilities. Sometimes statistics can be made to say what we want them to say, as Henry Dunlap, director of Children's Hospital in Los Angeles, wryly told me in observing he could demonstrate that "the number of hospital illnesses in children in Los Angeles is inversely proportional to the number of medical meetings out of town." Too, sampling the status quo for computer analysis is often a substitute for the vulnerable task of advancing new ideas, which, according to Dr. Jonas Salk, tend to go through three stages of acceptance: first, everyone says there's no truth in them; then, that there's some truth in them, but it's unimportant; and finally, that they're true and important, but everyone knew it all along.

Statistical profiles for brain handicap may tell us what exists — *if* statistics and data-gathering have been accurate, not biased — but they cannot create the innovation that answers the problem defined. So if society expects significant progress, it must cease regarding its innovators as troublesome simply because they are at variance with widely accepted but unworkable policies and procedures. And the various professions involved should understand that they are not always best able to police themselves, that sometimes outside help is needed to ensure objectivity and to avoid pressure from internal sources. Intelligent criticism, or the informed expression of an independent view, serves a useful purpose in the formation, exchange and evaluation of thought. Yet the prevalence of destructive criticism, or hatchet-jobbing for personal aggrandizement, has led to the view that *any* criticism is, by design and intent, subversive.

Recognition of variance also underlies recognition of developmental disabilities and the special individual differences of each and every one of us. Since we are all handicapped to some degree, in distinctly personal ways, any attempt to draw lines on the basis of degree undermines our essential humanity. With that fundamental recognition, there is much that we can do to cope, to understand and to help, thus becoming contributors to life rather than detractors from it.

If this seems to be an idealistic and hopeful view, well and good. Isn't it time that we began living in hope instead of fear, working for shared ideals instead of private advantage? Fear only begets more fear, just as anger begets more anger, and hatred more hatred. But love, let us remember, begets life, and forgiveness born of it can redeem anger, fear and hatred.

In addition to speeding public awareness and aiding the growth of new knowledge, we must also try to correct the lack of organization that has impeded the effective use of many valuable ideas. Lack of organization is implicated in situations characterized by the proliferation of conflicting operational routines and, conversely, personnel agitation over exceptions to or interruptions of established routine. Translating this into what can happen in programs for brain handicap, we start with a widely endorsed goal: to phase *out* institutional confinement to the extent possible and to phase *in* community living. Many skilled people then go to work in an effort to achieve this goal, but if there is poor organization at one or more levels, progress becomes tied up as each office issues its own set of regulations that may not be appropriately integrated with others. In some instances, those trying to reach objectives can find that what is approved at one place is disapproved elsewhere. Far better to remind ourselves that regulations are made for man, not man for regulations, and either limit the issuance of them to one agency or endeavor to ensure their consistency.

Instead of the emphasis on trying to cover every situation with a list of rules and requirements, it might be a simpler step in the right direction to give personality and performance tests to those interested in establishing community services. People who passed the test would be licensed as qualified to deliver care and permitted to proceed without taking endless orders. Most professionals, from lawyers to electricians, must take an examination to obtain a license to practice, after which they can set up business in the manner they choose. But there is *no* similar examination required of people offering out-of-home care in the intricate field of brain handicap, and the practitioner is further constrained by persistent supervision, when helpful inspection would suffice.

As in the beginning, parental participation preempts all other considerations — participation aimed not at extending dependence but at achieving as independent a life as possible for the developmentally disabled. After all the years of work, it may be hard for some parents to let go, to shift gears, to redirect their energies. That is the time when their work in community organizations will do most good for them and for society. Their wisdom and experience are needed to establish or improve activity centers, residential services and job opportunities, to advance and share information, offset fears, work for needed reforms in law, medicine, religion, education, industry and government — to increase understanding that makes the gift of life precious to all.

One question I hear repeatedly is, "Why help the brain-handicapped when so many others who aren't disabled need help and aren't getting it?" I would like to answer that the able are not only able, they are able to help themselves. The developmentally disabled need help to reach the point of being able to help themselves, and in the passage toward that end we improve the way in which we perceive each other, making a better society for everyone. To forget self is, I believe, to find self; to think only of self is to lose self.

Doctors aren't wrong. Teachers aren't wrong. Agencies aren't wrong. Parents aren't wrong. Mainly, we just haven't gotten together well enough — an omission that has led to disappointments and the errors born of misunderstandings. Another way is possible, and in it lies hope for the future of mankind. Up to the present, evolution has occurred through mutation based on genetic variety and adaptability. The next step stands to be manmade: through individual love and kindness eliminating hostility, raising the quality of using what we know, through all stages of child development, so that we may begin to realize the immense and as yet unfulfilled potential of each and every member of the Family of Man.

▣ Agencies

Parents and friends of the brain-handicapped can find assistance through various national organizations, some of which are listed below:

Division of Developmental Disabilities
Department of Health, Education, and Welfare
South Building, Room 3062
330 C Street, SW
Washington, D.C. 20201

National Institute of Mental Health
5600 Fishers Lane
Rockville, Maryland 20852

Developmental Disabilities Technical Assistance System
Suite 300, NCNB Plaza
Chapel Hill, North Carolina 27514

National Association for Retarded Citizens
2709 Avenue E East, Box 6109
Arlington, Texas 76011

Epilepsy Foundation of America
1828 L Street, NW, #406
Washington, D.C. 20036

National United Cerebral Palsy
Chester Arthur Building, #141
425 I Street, NW
Washington, D.C. 20001

National Society for Autistic Children
169 Tampa Avenue
Albany, New York 12208

Association for the Learning Disabled
Box 69
Albany, New York 12201

American Association on Mental Deficiency
5201 Connecticut Avenue, NW
Washington, D.C. 20015

Children's Division
American Humane Association
Box 1266
Denver, Colorado 80208

March of Dimes
1275 Mamaroneck Avenue
White Plains, New York 10602

National Association for Mental Health
10 Columbus Circle
New York, New York 10019

Easter Seal Society
2023 West Ogden Avenue
Chicago, Illinois 60604

Red Cross
17th and D Streets, NW
Washington, D.C. 20006

American Speech and Hearing Association
9030 Old Georgetown Road
Bethesda, Maryland 20014

Pilot Parents
Mrs. Zelda Gorlick
102 Heathrow Drive
Downsview, Ontario, M3M, 1X3
Canada

Each state also has a Department of Health and a Department of Education that maintain lists of local references.

◘ Recommended Reading

Among excellent works on specialized aspects of mental disabilities and human development, the following may be of added interest. To help the reader, titles are identified by general subject, presented informally and accompanied by brief descriptions. Degrees of authors have been omitted. No attempt has been made to rank according to relative importance.

AUTISM

Son-Rise — Barry N. Kaufman (New York: Harper & Row, 1976). The personal narrative of one family's success with infant sensory stimulation.

MENTAL RETARDATION

Challenges in Mental Retardation: Progressive Ideology and Services — Frank J. Menolascino (New York: Human Sciences Press, 1977). A study of trends, needs and issues.
Understanding the Mentally Retarded Child: A New Approach — Richard and Kathryn Jean Koch (New York: Random House, 1974). Causes of and programs in retardation.
The Exceptional Child Grows Up — Ernest Siegel (New York: E. P. Dutton & Co., 1975). Helping the retarded adolescent and young adult

EPILEPSY

Be Not Afraid — Robin White (New York: Dial Press, 1972). Fifteen-year story of the impact of epilepsy on a growing family.

CEREBRAL PALSY

Handling the Young Cerebral Palsied Child at Home — Nancie R. Finnie (New York: E. P. Dutton & Co., 1975). Illustrated practical guide on home management.

HYPERACTIVITY

Your Hyperactive Child — Gerald I. Sugarman and Margaret N. Stone (Chicago: Henry Regnery & Co., 1974). Answers many questions asked by parents and teachers.

APHASIA

The Shattered Mind — Howard Gardner (New York: Knopf, 1975). Reviews the breakdown of symbolic capacities following brain damage.
Aphasia in Children — Jon Eisenson (New York: Harper & Row, 1972). Treatment of children with language delays.

NUTRITION

Nutrition Against Disease — Roger J. Williams (New York: Bantam Books, 1973). The medical importance of cellular nutrition.
Malnutrition and Brain Development — Myron Winick (New York: Oxford University Press, 1976). Examines the impact of pre- and postnatal nutritional deficiencies on brain growth.
Improving Your Child's Behavior Chemistry — Lendon H. Smith (Englewood Cliffs, N.J.: Prentice-Hall, 1976). Strategies on raising happier children into healthier adults.
Orthomolecular Psychiatry — David Hawkins and Linus Pauling (San Francisco: W. H. Freeman & Co., 1973). *Growth and Development of the Brain: Nutritional, Genetic and Environmental Factors* — Mary A. B. Brazier, ed. (New York: Raven

Press, 1975). Scientific symposia documenting the direct relation between nutrition and brain biochemistry.

NEUROLOGY

Pediatric Neurology — Lester L. Lansky (Flushing, N.Y.: Medical Examination Publishing Co., 1975). Comprehensive resource for family physicians.

Living with Chronic Neurologic Disease — I. S. Cooper (New York: W. W. Norton & Co., 1976). Handbook for patients and families.

SOCIAL WORK

Chronic Illness in Children — Georgia Travis (Stanford: Stanford University Press, 1976). For those endeavoring to integrate community resources.

SEX

Human Sexuality and the Mentally Retarded — Felix de la Cruz and Gerald LaVeck (New York: Brunner/Mazel, 1973). Symposium on psychosexual development.

Sex Education and Counseling of Special Groups — Warren R. Johnson (Springfield, Ill.: Charles C Thomas, 1975). Sexuality for people with compounding difficulties.

Contraceptive Technology — *Various authors* (New York: Irvington Publishers, Halsted Division, John Wiley & Sons, 1976). Surveys all methods of contraception.

EARLY CHILDHOOD

Loving and Learning — Norma McDiarmid, Mari Peterson and James Sutherland (New York: Harcourt Brace Jovanovich, 1975). Infant stimulation from birth to age three.

The First Three Years of Life — Burton L. White (Englewood Cliffs, N.J.: Prentice-Hall, 1975). Stages of intellectual and emotional development.

The Natural Way to Raise a Healthy Child — Hiag Akmakjian (New York: Praeger, 1975). Psychological insights into childhood development.

Is Your Child's Speech Normal — Jon Eisenson (Reading, Mass.: Addison-Wesley, 1976). For parents: language development in children.

Infant Care — A. Frederick North, Jr. (New York: Arco, 1975). Parental guide to the newborn.

EDUCATION

Medical Problems in the Classroom — Raymond M. Peterson and James Cleveland (Springfield, Ill.: Charles C Thomas, 1975). A team approach for parents and professionals.

Helping Children Overcome Learning Difficulties — Jerome Rosner (New York: Walker & Co., 1975). Home teaching explained step by step.

Better Late Than Early — Raymond and Dorothy Moore (New York: Reader's Digest Press, 1975). Evidence that children are better off at home than at school until reaching an integrated maturity level.

How the Brain Works — Leslie A. Hart (New York: Basic Books, 1975). Indictment of education in terms of brain function and learning processes.

Normal Language Development — Carla Ross Trantham and Joan K. Pedersen (Baltimore: Williams & Wilkins, 1976). Diagnosis and therapy in language-disordered children.

The Myth of the Hyperactive Child — Peter Schrag and Diane Divoky (New York: Pantheon, 1975). The overuse of drugs by schools to effect child control.

The Logic of Action: Young Children at Work — Frances Pockman Hawkins (New York: Pantheon, 1974). Example of an outstanding teacher working with handicapped children.

Raising Children in Modern America — Nathan B. Talbot, ed. (Boston: Little, Brown & Co., 1976). In-depth symposium on the plight of children, along with projected solutions.

THE BRAIN

Brain and Behavior — Hugh Brown (New York: Oxford University Press, 1976). The importance of physiological psychology in relating all aspects of the brain.

Explaining the Brain — W. Ritchie Russell and A. J. Dewar

(New York: Oxford University Press, 1975). Introduction to the frontier of the mind.

In the Beginning: Your Baby's Brain Before Birth — Mortimer and Lynn Rosen (New York: New American Library, 1975). Brain development between conception and birth.

The Structure of Human Memory — Charles N. Cofer (San Francisco: W. H. Freeman & Co., 1976). Attempt to diagram how memory works.

PARENTS

Birth Without Violence — Frederick Leboyer (New York: Knopf, 1975). Techniques for easing trauma at birth.

When Children Need Help — David Melton (New York: Crowell, 1972). Guidance for parents of brain-handicapped children.

Parent-Infant Interaction — Ciba Foundation Symposium #33 (Elsevier, 1976). Influence of early interaction between mother and child.

The Joys and Sorrows of Parenthood — Group for the Advancement of Psychiatry (New York: Scribner's, 1973). Parental development and child raising.

What Now? A Handbook for New Parents — Mary Lou Rozdilsky and Barbara Banet (New York: Scribner's, 1975). Parent care during the early days of adjusting to a first child.

The Family Life of Sick Children — Lindy Burton (London: Routledge & Kegan Paul, Ltd., 1975). Ways in which parents cope with chronic childhood disease.

PSYCHOLOGY

Anger — Leo Madow (New York: Scribner's, 1972). Recognizing health problems from unexpressed anger.

Childhood Disorder — Philip Pinkerton (New York: Columbia University Press, 1975). Integrative psychosomatic approach in responding to early stress and emotional disorders.

The Myth of the Happy Child — Carole Klein (New York: Harper & Row, 1975). Natural geography of evolving childhood emotions.

The Second Sin — Thomas Szasz (Garden City, N.Y.: Doubleday, 1973). *The Myth of Mental Illness* — Thomas Szasz (New

York: Harper & Row, 1974). Iconoclastic discussions of conventional psychiatry.

The Psychology of Consciousness — Robert E. Ornstein (San Francisco: W. H. Freeman & Co., 1972). Theory of the brain's rational and intuitive functions in terms of hemispheres.

You Are Not Alone — Clara Claiborn Park and Leon N. Shapiro (Boston: Atlantic–Little, Brown, 1976). Comprehensive survey of mental illness.

Biographical Note

ROBIN WHITE, author of *Be Not Afraid*, the Harper Prize Novel *Elephant Hill* and other books, has had direct experience in the field of brain disabilities and child development since 1957. His articles on mentally handicapped children have appeared in many magazines, including *The Saturday Evening Post*, *Prism* (AMA), *National Wildlife* and *Early Years*, for which he received the Distinguished Achievement Award from the Educational Press Association of America. After serving as President of Parents and Friends of Retarded Citizens in Ft. Bragg, California, he was elected in 1973 to the Board of Trustees for California's four-county North Coast Regional Center, chairing Personnel for two years and voted President of the Board in 1975. In 1976, he was appointed Honorary State Chairman of *Read-a-thon* by the California Association for the Retarded, subsequently serving in 1977-1979 as NCRC liaison to the Area I Developmental Disabilities Board and to the State Association of Regional Center Agencies.